I0455463

Linger No Longer

A Memoir of Anorexia

Rae Swenson

Copyright: Rae Swenson 2009
All rights reserved.
ISBN: 1-4392-5941-0
ISBN-13: 9781439259412

Visit www.booksurge.com
to order additional copies.

Linger No Longer:
A Memoir of Anorexia

Rae Swenson

Dedicated to all those who struggle silently.

Acknowledgments

There are people that, without their help and encouragement, I would not have finished this book. I would like to thank my family for all their support, love and willingness to be a part of my life and this book, even the painful parts. My significant other, Benji, who has helped in every area of this project, and who continues to teach me and enrich my life with his love. Adele Warsinske, for generously giving her time to edit my manuscript, helping me through the process, and for sharing her wisdom. Lilium Pierson, for her valuable feedback. Vivienne Dutzar, my nutritionist and friend. Kent Hoffman, a mentor, teacher, and friend whose insight and wisdom has guided me through very dark periods of my recovery and my life. Austin Sawicki, your spirit is with me everyday and your love taught me so much.

Foreword

My recurring nightmare is that I have signed up for a class, have forgotten to attend and now must take the final exam. The experience of trying to help those who have been diagnosed with an eating disorder brings this recurring nightmare to mind.

The connection lies in the fact that despite my decades of work with people who struggle with disordered eating, never is there a day when I feel totally prepared. However, the endless variety of presentation of eating disorders fuels my fascination with the complexities of mind and body, as well as my energy to address the individuals with whom I have the privilege to come in contact. They are my teachers.

When my career in nutrition began to focus on the eating disorder spectrum, I was made aware that I could be taking a perilous detour, about to commit professional suicide. Countless people reminded me that this is a psychological disorder, that inappropriate eating behavior is only the symptom, that there is no place for a dietitian on the treatment team, and that I would be seen as a nut. Yet as I looked at the food choices, eating behaviors, and weight changes, common sense shouted that being at a nutritional disadvantage had to impair recovery from any illness. And so my journey into this mindboggling illness began. I find my life has been astoundingly enriched by my contact with those who are assaulted by eating disorders, and those who love and support them.

Many have written about their experience with anorexia or bulimia, but not all who write are enlightened or enlightening. Rae's beautifully written account of her illness and recovery is multidimensional. It is a humbling reminder of how much treatment providers see and don't see in their patients' process toward recovery.

Rae's very personal account allows us to view the many levels and countless paradoxes of this treacherous illness. She shares her exploration of herself, her complex love for her family, and her awareness of developmental and environmental factors that contribute to her illness. She prepares us for greater understanding of the illness by allowing us to feel her experience.

Eating disorders are now referred to as biopsychosocial ill-nesses and have been seen as such for many years by those who re-search them. Our culture, including – and sometimes especially – the healthcare community, is reluctant to accept that mind and body are not separate.

Although each eating disorder in each individual is a unique illness, one of the common features is the individual's lack of feeling of self-worth, and a need for a feeling of personal authenticity. A major enemy of recovery is a lay and medical community that labels an eating disorder as a behavior and refuses to acknowledge it as an illness, disregarding the growing body of evidence of the biological origin of this and other "mental" illnesses. The outcome is shortage of qualified health care professionals to participate in treatment, and a refusal of many reimbursement organizations to fund adequate treat-ment. The severity of this illness and the costs of treatment certainly could meet the definition of a catastrophic illness.

The serious financial hardship borne by families when no as-sistance is received may be mild compared to the tragic effect on those who struggle with this illness when they feel further invalidated by the indifference, or even malignant disregard of those who might treat them or assist with payment of costs of treatment.

Rae's account of her recovery and process of finding herself is a powerful reminder of what we have to lose if we do not help each other. I often tell my patients that if they all moved into recovery on the same day, there would be a dramatic shift in our universe. In their passionate and painful process of discovery of self, they inspire me to see more, feel more, learn more, and love more, admiring their cour-age to persevere. They are a window through which we can see more clearly the ills of our society, even as we learn from those with other diseases.

Walking through any illness with anyone can be painful. As people suffering from eating disorders enter into the recovery process, they learn the literal and figurative significance of nourishing oneself and one's soul. I am profoundly grateful for the nurturing they teach me. I am profoundly grateful to Rae for her presence in my life.

Vivienne Hamilton Dutzar, MS,RD

Linger no longer
My hell, my companion.
Your arms were cold,
But oh so inviting.
No more.
I felt the warmth
And though the chill still lingers,
I wish to be cold no more.
Here comes my life
And my arms are wide open.
No longer are my hands cemented
over my eyes.

-Journal Entry, June 1999

I
Childhood

I have many memories of my childhood, but the most defining, poignant memories I have are of the imaginary games and fantasies I used to create and act out every day. These games served as a crucial outlet for my self-expression, and they served an important purpose in my survival and development. When I look at my unique stories and reflect on how much they expressed my understanding of the world at that time, it is unsettling and validating all at once.

I did not have a particularly extraordinary childhood. Normal doesn't really equate with easy, but how I grew up probably doesn't stand out all that much. Normal is tricky this way. It doesn't really equal good, it just disguises the bad. It makes it easy for the observer to say, "Why did you end up with problems? You had such a normal life!" Yet, in all of my childhood's normal glory, there were some painful things I absorbed on a subtle, unspoken level.

My games meant a lot to me. I don't think there was anything particularly abnormal about them; they filled a need. There was something deeply satisfying in each one. I had several favorites that I played over and over, and they never lost their novelty or satisfaction for me. When I was in my stories, I felt happy, and somehow understood. They were an outlet for my true self. It's strange to go back to these stories as an adult; I feel exposed when I revisit them. Even then I knew they were secret, and to risk telling the secret was to risk being judged and to feel ashamed of what was an authentic expression of how I felt, what I longed for, and who I was—in some ways, who I still am.

A favorite story that I played as a 5-and 6-year-old even had a title: "Lost Children." I fantasized that I was a lost child. I was young, resilient, and strong. In the story, I had no family and I was alone, but this didn't scare me; in fact, I was happy. I was self-sufficient and spent my days foraging in a vast orchard that had everything I needed. I rotated from the cherries, to the apricots and plums, and eventually I ended up in the apples and pears as fall set in. No one knew where I was, and I liked this. My mom eventually had to get a dinner bell in order to summon me home from this game. I had a favorite cousin who was six months older than me. When he came to visit, I was happy to include him in this game.

I could include my cousin in this fantasy because I didn't feel as vulnerable as in some of the other stories. In this story I was strong, self-sufficient, and a survivor. I knew that on some level acting out these qualities could hardly be shameful, not in my family, and not in our culture. I was the ultimate individual, and I was happy. I didn't need anyone. I can't name a time or place when I didn't believe that mastering that façade was something to be proud of. The part of this game that is difficult for me to recognize is that I am still trying to be that quintessential "survivor." I am still deathly afraid of needing another. What felt so satisfying in my fantasy was that I didn't need anyone. It is far more painful to realize you do need someone and there's no one there. "Lost Children" was satisfying because there was no one there, and I didn't need them anyway. But the dinner bell always rang, calling me back.

In a more vulnerable fantasy, one that I played a lot but did not tell anyone about, I was a princess in a castle, but only I knew I was a princess. To everyone else, I was a servant. I was mistreated, bossed around, and ignored. I knew that someday I would escape and this helped me get through the days and remain compliant to the demands of the horrible, rich family that tortured me. I always had hope that I would have my own life far away from the dreadful palace where I was imprisoned. I would not allow myself to be defeated. In the fantasy, I met a wonderful friend and he visited me every day. We escaped together on particularly terrible days and I could go back to the palace invigorated, hopeful, and unafraid.

For this story I would dress in ragged old dresses and imagine the setting of an early nineteenth-century lifestyle. This was probably based on one of the many Rodgers and Hammerstein musicals to which my father routinely subjected me. No matter which musical it was, the women always had these amazing skirts. For some reason it was appealing to me to have to grapple with and trip over a skirt as I was being admonished by my evil master. Another factor that created the perfect setting for my story was the secluded farmhouse we lived in, miles away from town. This helped create an authentic feeling of imprisonment. The farmhouse was old, and the collection of enormous trees in the backyard dated it. There was a particularly wonderful willow tree that created a haven under its branches. When I escaped from the castle, this was my retreat. It was magical, mysterious, and quiet. This was a game I always played alone.

Part of the secrecy of this game was that unlike the "lost child" role, being the servant in this game held some shame for me. As the servant I was still surviving, but I was in need of someone. I was sad, and the aloneness was not glorified and wonderful—it was terrible. This was a part of myself I wanted to hide, and I cannot remember a time that feeling dependent or depressed was not a source of shame. Even now, I retreat from people I love when I feel this, probably from fear that they may see that I need them, which would be the ultimate vulnerability and shame for me. The servant girl represented unabashed neediness, despair, and abandonment. In this story, I tried valiantly to survive and make the best of it, but in my real life, I didn't even acknowledge to myself that I felt this, let alone allow someone else to know about these shameful feelings.

The next fantasy was a bit more reality based. You could call it modeling to a certain extent. This story involved a busy mother (this part played by me) dragging her poor, compliant, and well-behaved daughter around as she frantically tried to get everything done. There were times that I needed others to have a part in my stories. Unfortunately for my younger cousin, she was an easygoing, compliant four-year-old, and I used this to my advantage in order to fully act out the frantic mother role. The game usually began with my firmly grabbing my cousin's upper arm, and saying, "Let's play house." She caught on eventually, but there were a few glorious times when bribery was not needed. The game looked very much like everyday life. I needed to get to the grocery store, meet my friends, go to a job interview, clean the house, etc. Each errand was interrupted by a more urgent, important errand, and as the day grew more frantic, the grip on my cousin's arm grew increasingly stronger. My somewhat composed, in-control self degenerated into a distracted, bossy, and chaotic whirlwind. Of course, my cousin quickly grew weary of the game as any self-respecting person would do, which was all the more reason for me to retain a vise-like grip on her upper arm. I was not usually bossy and controlling, but there was something deeply satisfying in playing this character for me.

This isn't to convey a false impression of my mom. One might be suspecting some sort of rough treatment in my homelife, but this was not the case at all. In fact, even spankings were a rarity. The part that reflected reality was that my mother was a busy person with a couple of other kids besides me. She wasn't bossy or abusive like the character in this fantasy, but she was distracted. I remember my mother in our home much like one would imagine a mouse in a maze. She was always moving, turning this way and that, somewhat unpredictable in the way she worked down her list of chores, never stopping until she reached the goal. Although, come to think of it, she never reached the goal because the tasks were was never ending. In her defense, she was usually the only one taking care of the house, the dinner, the people, and so on.

In the last story, I am dying. The way in which I died would vary, given the day. But, it was always something long and drawn out to give me time to savor the moment. Sometimes it was cancer, and I was lying weakly in a hospital bed bidding my family farewell as the last moments of my life lingered. Other times I was in a terrible accident, paralyzed and in a wheelchair. At the time, I assumed that wheelchairs would most likely result in death. The most fascinating and wonderful part of this story was watching everyone who loved me gather around. I comforted them while basking in the attention. I was strong and brave because I knew how loved I was, and it made dying worth it. It was intoxicating to imagine these people, hit with the blow of my disappearing forever, realizing how they had taken me for granted. I imagined that they felt sorry and horribly ashamed of how they had neglected to see what an important part of the family I was. I was actually the youngest child at the time that I frequently played out this fantasy, but I feel like I should have been a middle child. I later had a younger sister when I turned ten, which validated this feeling.

The story spoke to my feelings of being invisible, easy to ignore. I think to my child's mind it meant that I wasn't that important. I developed a habit of weighing how interesting what I had to say was, and many times I ended up not saying anything at all because I often concluded that even if it were interesting (which it probably wasn't) someone else had something more interesting to say. This could have been why I spent so much time alone, although I can't say that conclusively.

I had another fear that didn't help this feeling of insignificance. I couldn't stand to get in trouble. I hated it. I felt very bad about myself if I were even slightly reprimanded. I made sure to always follow the rules. In truth, I never got in trouble because I was frightened by the thought of it. I hated to disappoint or cause conflict with people, even perfect strangers. I guess you could say I engaged in non-attention seeking behaviors, which didn't work out so well given that what I really wanted was attention.

As I put these stories together, I can begin to see how I tried to fit in a complex family system. My mother was the busy mother that I acted out in my game; she was always trying to keep everyone and everything happy and functional. She was nurturing and made sure that we had what we needed. She was also in constant motion. I felt somewhat deprived emotionally because it was so difficult to get someone to sit down and be present with me. All through my childhood, when I was upset about something, I would retreat to my room and sit on my bed or in the closet and wait. I didn't usually cry, but I always felt like I was going to explode. I waited, hoping that my mom would come in and talk to me. She rarely did. As an adult, I told her about this, and her response was apologetic. She said, "Rae, I always thought you didn't need me. I didn't realize that's what you wanted." I know that's the truth for my mom, and I see that I played an important role in this. I was the youngest of three children, and I think it was a lifesaving belief for my mom to think that one of her children was highly independent. I feel sad that my mom and I "missed" each other in this way.

This feeling of needing someone, yet knowing on some level that I needed to be independent, showed up in my stories. On the one hand, I was a servant girl—abandoned, alone, and needy. On the other hand, when I played "Lost Children," I was self-sufficient and I didn't need anyone—a denial of feeling abandoned. All the while, deep down, I was quietly hating the whole game, jumping from abandoned despair to forced self-reliance.

The other dynamic was that I always felt less important than my older sister. She had this way of getting my mother's attention and I was jealous of that. She was expressive. If she was upset, she made sure that she got it out. She was like my dad. They were both good at what my mom called "venting." If there was a crisis, or someone had something to say, my mom would listen. I was more like my mom. We never said much about our feelings unless someone pulled it out of us. The dying story really speaks to this feeling. I wanted to feel significant enough that people would sit down with me and listen. I believed that a crisis was needed in order for this to happen—that I, alone, didn't merit that kind of attention.

Often, I felt very lonely in my family, like I was outside looking in, hoping they would notice me. In other ways, I felt like the presence of my family was overwhelming. There was always a sense of unpredictable boundaries. Sometimes there was very little space and other times, the distance felt immense.

Little girls grow up, and I did too. I stopped spending time in my fantasies, but they remained a part of me. They were always there. They enabled me to be myself in a slightly removed setting so that what I was feeling and experiencing wasn't quite so painful. I may have stopped pretending, but the stories were channeled into another form as I moved into adolescence. Then a new, compelling way to express myself found its way into my heart and mind.

II
The Voice

"The Voice" is my term for the companion that invaded my presence and turned my mind into a painful, tumultuous battleground. Some people call it "negative mind," or they give it names, like "Jezebel the Seductress," or "the devil." Whatever the name, I think everyone who has an eating disorder becomes intimately acquainted with what I call "the Voice." It's there to cheer you on when everyone else is crying, "Stop!" It's there to remind you how fat you are, what an ugly person you are, and to question every positive step forward.

The Voice gradually slipped into my mind and took up residence, snaking its roots through everything I thought and did. Really, the Voice deserves a better name. For years, the Voice held a higher status in my world than God did, had I really believed in God at the time. But I can't possibly think of renaming the Voice now. In fact, I suppose I don't want to attribute human-like qualities to it. Maybe to leave it an it makes it more separate, less powerful. I have to take every opportunity I can to make it less powerful, because powerful it was and still can be.

I cannot really remember a time without the Voice. I cannot recall how I used to think about food or myself before anorexia. I know that gradually my thoughts became more distorted, and my relationship with food turned into a game of control fraught with shame. Somehow, in the course of the summer between my sophomore and junior years of high school, it seemed like whatever had been lurking beneath the surface in my soul exploded and nothing remained the same.

We moved to Spokane when I was fourteen. I have always been slow to transition. Every time we moved, it took months for me to overcome my shyness and make friends. I was always slightly depressed for the first year, and this move was no different, except that this time the change was more drastic: larger school, fewer siblings around, and my adolescence to contend with. Given that I was not very vocal about my feelings, I had to find outlets–grown up, acceptable outlets–not escaping into childish fantasies. Cross-country proved to be the perfect such outlet that year. I had always played sports. In small towns, playing sports was a person's only insurance against becoming a social outcast. I had survived many moves to small towns through sports, beginning in the second grade with Saturday morning basketball.

The only problem was that a big school has team tryouts. This posed another risk. What if I tried out and was cut from the team? That was a path to rejection. However, the one team that actually needed members and was not holding tryouts was the cross country team. I joined the team, having never run over two miles consecutively. Running quickly became my relief from feeling out of place and lonely.

My first day of school was terrifying. I walked into school and the crowds of people assaulted my senses. I had no idea that many people my age actually existed. Up to that point, I had lived in towns where the entire population did not exceed the enrollment at my new high school. However, what was particularly surprising was that, despite its size, everyone seemed to know each other. As I walked into the front doors a sea of people loomed before me. They were all grouped into small little clusters that I would later realize were very definite cliques to be negotiated with caution. No one seemed to be looking for someone to talk to. My impression was that these people, much like the people in the small towns we had moved to and from, had known each other most of their lives, and the social scene I was walking into was well established. Once again, I was an outsider looking at how to break in, or at least survive. But this time, there was no recess, no game to join, and I was anonymous in this mass of people. I felt nauseated and utterly terrified. It is an awful feeling to have to pretend that you have something to do, somewhere to be, someone to talk to when in fact you don't. I drifted around dying for the first period bell to ring, aching to end the awkward moments of clearly having no one to talk to while everyone else was mingling with friends they had not seen all summer.

The bell did ring, bringing relief, but I soon realized that class was just as alienating with less anonymity. Everyone was vying for seats by their friends, a few people staring at me cautiously. I felt the intensity of insecurity both in myself, and in everyone around me. The social atmosphere created by adolescents is something phenomenal. I felt like I had no tools for navigating this situation and each quiet, un-approachable stare heightened my discomfort. I responded by pulling further into myself. I remember the chorus of a Simon and Garfunkel song going through my head, "I am a rock. I am an island." That's how I felt. I was aching inside for someone to talk to me because I knew I wouldn't have the courage to approach anyone myself. I waited, my face blank in an attempt to hide my fear.

After school on that first day, I walked into the practice room at the end of my rope, with tears threatening to come and embar-rass me even more. The coach sent everyone on an "outrun" that day, which meant that we went running for 30 to 40 minutes with a few other team members. I ran with a girl who was only going for 30 minutes, as I did not want to embarrass myself by not being able to finish the run. The girl was a freshman. She was a bit eccentric, but in a way that drew people to her rather than making her a social outcast. I learned that she was actually not that into cross-country, but she had been coerced by her older brother to try it. We plodded along down the road, and as I ran, the tension from the day began to drain out of me. I felt like nothing mattered when I ran. My breathing drowned out my thoughts, and the physical challenge pushed my emotional pain into the corners of my mind. By the end of the run, I felt better, a lot better. That was my first experience of having a "runner's high." Every day after that, I looked forward to practice, knowing that no matter how bad the day was, running would make it seem better.

In the first month of cross-country, I made friends with sev-eral of my teammates. It quickly became apparent that this group belonged to a clique that was on the fringes of the school's popular clique. They were trying hard to make it to the inner circle of the popular clique, and this involved a variety of experimentation and risk taking that could result in two very different outcomes: either the group would become part of the cherished inner circle or they would veer towards the outside even more. It seemed that there was not much rhyme or reason to how this would turn out, except that if the group was to be popular, they definitely had to be good at sports, and none of them were. The writing was probably on the wall at that point, but I wasn't familiar enough with the scene to see it. I wasn't quite sure if I cared about being popular, but I was afraid of the alternative. It seemed as if they were on a path to trouble—something I had avoided my whole life.

They began to experiment with drinking and partying, which I followed along with at first. Among the memories of this time, there are several indelible moments. One of these moments was the first time I drank alcohol. We went to a friend's house, and I lied to my mother saying that we were going to a late movie and I would spend the night with my friend, Ashley. Over the course of the night I narrowly missed losing my virginity to a boy five years older than I was. I got high for the first time, and woke up on my friend's living room floor, sleeping next to her three dogs. I drove home that morning disgusted with myself and horrified. There was not a single redeeming moment to the night that I could remember. Every memory that crossed my mind made me shudder. Yet, I didn't walk away, because I feared having to drift around the school as I had for the first few weeks with no one to talk to, no group to sit with at lunch, feeling uncomfortably self-conscious.

So, I continued to follow along. We would run to someone's house during our outrun days at practice and take vodka shots from the liquor cabinet, then run back to school. We had slumber parties and got drunk while locked in our bedrooms under the guise of watching movies. It all felt terrible, and I knew that at some point I would have to find the courage to walk away.

The courage finally came toward the end of spring my sophomore year. One of my friend's parents went on a trip for the weekend, and someone's mother covered for us while we threw a party at the vacant house. Around one o'clock that morning, I was standing in the bathtub with my fully clothed and passed out friend, desperately hosing her down with cold water trying to wake her up and clean up the puke. As I stood there I felt so afraid. I hated this kind of life, and my revulsion was so tangible at that moment that I knew I would never be able to do this again. In that moment, I saw my goals slipping away. I imagined what would happen to me if the police found out or if I somehow managed to get pregnant during a thoughtless night. I hated how I felt about myself when I was around this group. I felt like a liar. I felt fake and stupid. I had spent the year feeling disgusted with myself and uncomfortable with the people I called my friends. Finally, when the summer came and I did not have to face going to school every day, I stopped calling them and hanging out with them. I isolated myself and worked at my summer job in an attempt to fill the loneliness and depression that lurked beneath the surface.

III
The Voice Creeping In

It was the summer after this year when my thinking began to change. I worked as a lifeguard at a small neighborhood pool for the summer. The memories of that summer are very vivid, but I cannot pinpoint when I began to change. It was a very hot summer. The dry heat felt like an assault on my entire system. I dreamt wistfully of big department stores with air conditioning that was so cold it had the ability to make you shiver, even on those 100 degree days. My time was spent sitting by a pool full of kids, scanning from shallow end to deep end and back again. It was my summer job, and I had learned to hate it. It was like having a ball and chain attached to my foot for six to eight hours a day, five days a week. I was always sitting, always scanning, while the glare of the sun shot into my eyes as it reflected off the water.

All of me felt lazy and unmoving: my mind, my body, and my spirit. In the course of the summer I found things to think about, things that busied my mind and made up for what was lacking in my spirit. They were silly little mathematical games, like counting the tiles on the classroom ceiling just so time might go by faster. I trained hard that summer for the coming cross-country season. I had been voted team captain for that fall and I took the position seriously. It was also a way to distract myself from what I considered my utter failures in terms of choices the previous year. Thus, I set a goal to run 350 miles before the end of the summer, and I kept a log of the miles I ran.

Keeping track of my running became my little game. I thought about the miles that I had ran every week. I imagined the routes, added up the miles, and calculated my speed. I thought of what I ate each day and compared the calories burned during my run with the number of calories I consumed. Of all the things to think about, I cannot say why I chose this. I once read in a magazine that a person burned roughly 100 calories for every mile they ran. This little tidbit of information gave me something real to calculate, a way to check my progress and gauge my accomplishments. It was safer to think about this than my failure to feel connected with others, or the impending school year. My game was innocent at first; I was just trying to fill the time. I would scan the pool, look at the clock, and plan where to run that night when I got off work.

When thinking and calculating was no longer enough, I developed another ritual. As I scanned the pool, I did toe raises by the pool, counting to fifty each time I did them. After toe raises, I did squats, then walked the length of the pool a few times. I did this little routine whenever sitting got to be too much. Really, I did it whenever the thought of how many calories I was *not* burning bombarded my mind and started to ruin my concentration on the pool. I could not stand to sit still and if I was, my mind was racing. I became so full of anxiety when I wasn't burning calories that there were times I felt as if I couldn't breathe.

When I was not working at the pool, I gradually found myself turning down invitations to go to the movies or do things with my friends if it interfered with my exercise schedule. Everything became second to running. My weight started dropping rapidly. This change went unnoticed by me until it started being acknowledged by my co-workers or the people who frequented the pool. Unbeknownst to me, my mother was watching silently, yet observantly. I recall one conversation I had with her around the middle of that July. I told her how good I felt and that I had lost sixteen pounds. She said, "That's fine Rae. You look good, just don't lose anymore."

"Oh no, of course not." I replied. However, in my head, I was thinking, *maybe just a few more pounds and I'll feel even better*. I was already entering a state of euphoria from not eating that was even better than my runner's high. It felt so good. I was beginning to depend on these states to keep myself from falling into depression.

It was during this time that the Voice started to emerge. The Voice was not an actual voice with a sound of its own, rather it was a voice within my head that somehow had broken away from me and formed a will of its own. It gradually became more and more separate from my other thoughts, yet I did not quite recognize its force until I started to battle with it.

At some point during that summer, my counting game took on another dimension. Suddenly, the calories I ate could not exceed the calories I burned running. I could not justify eating if I did not run. Whenever I did eat without running or ate more than I burned, I would get upset. At first, I would be a little irritated with myself. But, as time went on, I would get unreasonably upset. It would paralyze me. I think this is where the Voice started to emerge with a mind of its own. It would beat me up. I know it was myself, my own thoughts, but at the same time it felt so removed. It was like boot camp: the Voice was the officer yelling at me while I was the little, snot-nosed brat he was trying to make into a soldier. It was always there to torture me when I thought I had messed up, and it seemed like I messed up at every turn. Oftentimes, the feeling of failure was so thick it was suffocating.

Physically, I felt lighter, harder, and stronger as I lost weight. It was an intoxicating, addicting sensation, as if I could walk on air. My clothes became more than loose; they were baggy. I could pull my once fitted jeans off without unzipping them. I even noticed the way my ankles and wrists became smaller. My bones began to protrude more, and my skin seemed more taut as it stretched over my bones. At first, I was intensely aware of every part of my body as the weight came off. Yet, the more weight I lost, the easier it became to forget my body altogether. I did not feel the clothes on my body—they simply hung on me. I rarely felt the weight of my arms or legs, for there was not much left to carry. When I stood with my feet together, I did not even feel my legs touch; they were too thin.

I reached a place where I could examine my body in the mirror like it was no longer a part of who I was. I could identify every part that looked chubbier, every part that had a little too much flesh. Gradually, my mind and body became so separate that I rarely made the connection that my body was part of me. Granted, I could look in the mirror and see my face and know it was part of me, but my body was not part of who I was. It was a casing, a tool. I needed to keep it looking perfect, polished, trim, and hard. My body was a machine with no feelings. It operated rain or shine, exhausted or not. Really, it was less than a machine because I did not even give it the respect a machine deserved. I punished it. Every flaw, real or imagined, was a justification for all of the abuse I subjected my body to physically as well as the mental abuse the Voice showered upon it.

I adjusted my daily schedule to fit the demands of the Voice. Rather than spending time with friends, I would stay home and weed the garden, or clean the house for my mother who was working full-time. I loved to cook. I would cook anything for anybody, but I never ate what I cooked. I made my father and little sister lunch and breakfast every day that I could. It made me feel better to take care of others. I felt worthy of life for at least one reason. Somehow, by feeding them, I was feeding myself. When I was hungry, I turned to magazines or cookbooks packed with recipes. By the time the summer had ended, I had lost even more weight, and I was truly obsessed. However, I didn't notice that my thoughts were strange. Of course, I never voiced them out loud; I assumed they were normal. I never questioned my actions or habits. My thoughts had slowly morphed into an illogical obsession, but, as surprising as it may seem, I remained unaware that there was a problem.

The end of the summer came and I had to face school again. Cross-country practice started a week before school, and some of my teammates who had not seen me all summer were openly surprised at my appearance. Many of them commented. My coach told me I looked great and that she could not wait to see how much my times had improved over the summer. I immediately felt the pressure start to weigh on me, but even as the expectations caused my anxiety to heighten, I was pleased that everyone had so much faith in me. I led the team on runs with the other team captains, designed workouts for several of our practices, and started running harder as the stress of school got to me.

I enrolled in several Advanced Placement courses and ran for the position of ASB secretary. It seemed that everything in my life had become a test, a performance to show others that I was not a failure. I spent a great deal of time studying, working as hard as I could to maintain the perfection to which I clung. For me, there was no room for error. Error meant failure. Somehow, running remained a release for me even as the competition was yet another stress, another test to see whether I would fail or not. All the while, my mother was silently watching me, and before anyone else knew what was happening, she was aware that something was wrong. Eventually, she addressed the problem, much to my shock and dismay.

During track season the previous spring I had sprained my ankle, and a few weeks into the school year my mom suggested that I go to the doctor before cross-country races started, just to make sure it had healed okay. I agreed and she came to the appointment with me. I thought nothing of it until she wanted to come into the room with me. When the doctor arrived, she asked him how much I weighed. Startled by this question, I looked at her, speechless. Weight had never been something she emphasized with me. We rarely spoke of weight or body image. Sure, she was a bit of a health-food junkie, but beyond this food and weight were not a large focus for our family. When the doctor told her that I weighed 109 pounds, she told him that she was worried about me because at the beginning of the summer I had weighed around 130 pounds.

The doctor specialized in sports medicine and was quite familiar with seeing cross-country runners who weighed very little. He told my mother not to worry, that I was running a lot and weight loss was expected; then he asked me if I was eating right. Of course I was eating right, I told him defensively. I was shocked that my mother worried about my weight and my eating habits. I walked out of the doctor's office angry with her. It was as if she had tried to ruin my success, and worst of all, she had been underhanded about it. I could not understand why she had done this. It felt so invasive.

I felt good at that point. Everything felt manageable when I had so much control over my eating. I had reached a point where I very rarely broke the food regimen I had set for myself. I ate about as many calories as I ran off each day. I could not justify more than that. I think it was the control that made me feel good. It was like all my ducks were in a row when I stuck to my diet plan. I did not think of it as restriction, or a conventional diet. I saw it as discipline, and I believed it strengthened me when I could stick to this sort of regime. That night, I asked my mom why she had done what she did in the doctor's office. In reply, she told me that she was concerned about me and asked me if I would go see a counselor, just to make sure that I was okay. Angry, and in an attempt to prove her wrong, I agreed.

To appease my mother, two weeks later I went to an appointment she had set up for me. The counselor asked me a lot of questions. I remember only one. She asked, "What do you want to weigh?" I remember telling her I wanted to weigh about 115 pounds, but it was hard to hold that weight with all of the running that I did. Even at the time, I remember feeling like I was half lying. I think I knew I could maintain that weight, but I didn't have the desire. Really, I wanted to weigh nothing, zero. The counselor gave me a questionnaire to fill out and send to her before we met again. It asked questions like: Do you worry about your weight? Do you try to please others a lot? Do you throw up after meals? Again, in an attempt to make my mother believe I was okay, I completed the questionnaire and sent it to the counselor.

At my next appointment, she told me I was at high risk for anorexia nervosa, but I was not anorexic. I walked triumphantly out of the office with the results that would prove to my mother that I was fine. Three weeks later I had lost another five pounds.

IV
Evasive Clarity

While the change in my mind was gradual and undetected, there came a moment when I realized that my thoughts were no longer normal. I had just finished a cross-country race. It was a Saturday, and I planned to stay the night with my sister who, at the time, was a sophomore in college. She went to a nearby university, and my visits to her dorm were often the highlights of my week. My mother and younger sister dropped me off, and my sister and I planned to have a slumber party that night.

We went to our favorite drive-in and bought peanut butter milkshakes. I, of course, had not eaten all day in preparation for the "treat" I knew I would have with my sister. Even so, I felt like hell as I drank it. As I enjoyed it, the now familiar Voice in my head kept me from being able to justify why I even deserved this sort of treat. So, after successfully finishing the shake and feeling awful for it, I changed into my pajamas, hoping to pass out so that I didn't have to listen to the Voice and the extreme discomfort in my shrunken belly. That is when it happened. I lost it. Something broke in me. Maybe it happened at the right time, just when I was struggling with that nagging Voice and hating it. Whatever the case, when I heard my sister gasp behind me as I was changing into my pajamas, it all became real.

"Rae, oh my God, have you seen your back?"

"What do you mean?"

"You've lost so much weight, your back looks sick. You can see every bone."

I turned around to face her and I could see the horror in my sister's face as we stood in her dorm room. Her horror touched me in a spot that was becoming untouchable. So, where I usually would have ignored her comment, instead I listened. I turned in front of the mirror and glimpsed my back. My shoulder blades stuck out and I could see the point of each vertebra in my spine as it poked against my taut skin. I felt strangely disconnected from the picture in the mirror. Was that *my* back? It no longer felt like a part of me; my mind and body were oddly separate from each other. For a brief moment, I saw the connection, maybe through my sister's eyes, and it occurred to me that even if I wanted to eat more, I could not somehow. I crumpled to the floor and started crying.

"I don't know what's wrong with me. I can't eat anymore. I can't make myself--I really can't make myself eat anymore."

For some reason, the prison I had become locked in became apparent and real to me at that moment. I had never noticed I was looking through bars when I looked out the window until that moment with my sister. And while the insight was fleeting, the impact of it lingered in my mind and haunted me when quiet moments came. I was a prisoner inside my head, trapped by an obsession that had taken control of me when I was not looking. I felt tricked and robbed of myself at times. I was truly imprisoned by something larger than myself, and try as I might, the cell seemed inescapable. I could not recall when it had happened. There was no date, no event to which I could trace my strange way of thinking.

It had never occurred to me that something was strange until that moment in my sister's dorm room, when I realized that I was no longer making the choice not to eat. Rather, I was no longer *allowed* to eat. Of course, if someone had asked me who had made that rule, I would not have felt right answering that it was myself. I knew it would be one of those questions that a counselor would ask to make her client think. I could hear the conversation in my head.

"Rae, who told you that you couldn't eat? Who made that rule?"

"I don't know," and for lack of a better answer, combined with the counselor's expectant look, I would hesitantly answer, "myself, I guess." Yet, the minute the words came out, I would know that my answer was wrong somehow, and I would quickly try to correct myself. I mean, how dumb would that be? "Yes, counselor, I told myself I couldn't eat, and so I am starving myself to death...." What sense would that make? So, I would try to fix my answer, "I mean, *I* didn't make that rule. It just..." *It just what?* "Well it just sort of happened. I don't know how or when, but it's there and I can't eat and--and," and my words would trail off because what else could I say?

The rules that were in my head had taken on a life of their own. It was no longer me, but a monster living inside my head. It was there to tell me when I messed up. It was there beating me up when the last thing I needed was criticism. It was there loud and clear, telling me not to eat, when it had been days since my last skimpy meal. And I listened. Not because I wanted to, but because it was so strong, so powerful that it never crossed my mind to argue with it. It became "the Voice," and it was my companion, my constant critic. It did not care if I wanted it to go away. It would not. Recovery was not about learning how to eat, it was about learning how to battle the damn Voice.

I knew how to eat. I even enjoyed food. I looked forward to the small meals I could eat, but that was it. I had to be allowed to eat it. I was allowed to eat half of a non-fat muffin in the morning, so I could enjoy that. But, if I ate any more than that in the morning, I was down for the count. I would not be able to focus all morning. I would feel like crap and all I would be able to think about was the extra food I had eaten. If I could "fix" it at lunchtime by not eating, then it would be okay, and I would be able to focus for the afternoon. If not, things got really bad. I would sit in class distracted, writing lists of calories and adding them up over and over again. I would think of all the ways I could make up for my crime. It was like I was in negotiations for my life, for my self-esteem.

You weak-willed, stupid girl, why did you eat so much this morning? Now you're going to have to make up for it. You're going to have to prove that you actually do have discipline. You are really disgusting, do you know that?

"Oh God, I did eat too much. I ate so much. I won't eat at lunchtime, so the extra 200 calories will be made up then. I can't eat at lunch."

I hope you can do it. You probably won't be able to do it. You're going to be really tired by cross-country practice, but you better not eat. Come on, prove to me that you're not weak. This is your chance to make it all better.

"I know, I know. I was weak. I can't believe I did that this morning. Never again. Maybe I won't eat lunch or dinner today." My "make-up" plans were always very harsh. You see, I had to compensate for a lot more than calories eaten; I had to punish myself for screwing up in the first place. It was my desperate attempt at making myself perfect again.

It was torture inside my head. It took such an effort to direct my thoughts in a way other than this. All the budgeting, the obsessing. The "take-here-and-give-there" game that constantly ran through my mind was all-consuming. It was never far from my awareness, and the worst part was that it had me in its grasp. I had no control over it. That is the deceiving part of an eating disorder. A person feels in total control. I felt powerful and full of iron will. To my mind, I possessed an amazing amount of self-discipline. Then, gradually, as my energy waned and my spirit began to disappear behind the lists of nutrition facts clouding my mind, I realized that the Voice had control over me, not the other way around.

Only after I began to glimpse this realization did I agree to go to a nutritionist. And yet, clarity never remained. I visited the nutritionist once a week and whenever I walked into her office, I would instantly be annoyed. I could not believe what was happening; the whole business felt like such a big deal about nothing. My annoyance would mount when I was asked to get on the scale. As I stepped on, the nutritionist would always stop me and ask me to take off my shoes and coat. I felt like some sort of animal that gets weighed in at the fair to see if it was worthy to sell. I would watch carefully as she slid the weights into position, and then I would tuck the information carefully away in my mind. She had me keep food records and come every week. I did. I hated it. It was invasive. It was like turning in my diary every week for someone to read and critique it. I knew my eating would not be satisfactory and she would scold me in the way that only doctors can. I lost my privacy. I felt like an animal in the spotlight, and I was always fighting the stranger spotlighting me, staring my newest foe down, daring him to try and stop me.

I often lied on my food records just to protect what little privacy I had. Of course, I could never decide whether to say I had eaten more or less than I actually had. It was almost too much shame to tolerate when I exaggerated. I would think about what a pig I would look like. I would imagine my nutritionist looking at the records, then looking at me and thinking, "No wonder she's so fat, look at how much she eats." Then there was the logical part of me that knew she would see I was lying. A lot of times I wanted to make my records look like I had eaten less. It was painful to write the list of food that I ingested each day. It disgusted me that I even had to eat at all. It was awfully difficult to be honest, and it was even harder to decide which way to lie.

Every now and then, clarity would come and the idea of death would keep me up at night. I would lie awake with fear freezing my thoughts and my breath. My heart would get jumpy with anxiety. I would see my twiggy limbs for what they were–signs of a quickly disappearing body. Clarity usually slipped away as quickly as it came, like an elusive ghost. I could not hold on to it.

While I had promised my mother to see a nutritionist once a week, knowing deep down that I needed to get better, during the majority of the appointments I was convinced that the lady was utterly mad in her requests of me. She told me to drink protein shakes with whole milk and make my portions bigger. *Yeah right lady, whatever you say.*

"When is cross-country over?" she asked me one day. I told her it would be over in four weeks. "Do you have to finish?"

Was she crazy? "Of course," I told her.

"You need to stop running after that."

What was she talking about? No way! How could I do that?! In my mind I saw myself puffing up like a balloon, and I felt my body start to shake. "Umm, I don't think so," I told her.

She instructed me to try harder with my food records and to come back the next week. If I started doing better, maybe I could keep running. I wore overalls and a sweater to my next appointment thinking they might up my dwindling weight by a few pounds, and every pound counted. It didn't help. She told me it was no longer a choice—my failure to gain any weight showed I wasn't trying, and I *had* to stop running when cross-country ended. The thought made me feel sick; it kept me up at night wondering what I would do if I could not run. As I did with everything they told me, I disregarded their threats because I did not believe they would come true. Everyone was overreacting. It was not me, it was them—plain and simple.

Their threats of imminent death always managed to sneak into my thoughts when quiet moments came. Then the fear and doubt came. I oscillated between the fear of death and the fear of gaining weight. Sometimes I knew I was sick, yet as I sat watching my friends eat lunch, I was perfectly convinced that I was the strongest person on earth. Somehow, I had escaped human weakness. I did not feel hunger, I did not need food, and even if I wanted it, I had the strength to refuse it—unlike anyone else. In saying this, it is important to note that I never had the feeling that I deserved to eat lunch like everyone else either. Not eating was not just about strength; it was my punishment. My punishment for what, I do not know exactly. I just knew that somehow I was a failure. Everyone else deserved to eat; I did not. Food was my foe, and I was desperately trying to win the war. Food ruined everything. It ruined my strength, my concentration, and my life. In this world of mine, I was fighting a war that no one was aware of except me. This was my state of mind for the majority of the time.

So, despite occasional clarity, I continued on with my routine. I ran twice a day, as much as I could. I began my day by mindlessly rolling out of bed and slipping on my running shoes before I had time to think about how tired I was. I ran at practice after school, dreading it a bit more every day because my exhaustion was almost unbearable. I ended my day thinking about where I would run the next morning, how far, and what I would eat afterwards. However, as the end of the cross-country season neared, I was filled with both dread and relief. The nutritionist was adamantly sticking to what she said, and I knew the running had to end, but I knew I could not end it myself. I ended my season with a personal record, beating the top girl on our team.

Instead of feeling proud and happy, I remember hugging my opponent and team member and crying. Crying out of relief that it was over, crying because my victory left me feeling empty and horribly mean. It was supposed to be the happy climax of my high school running career, but instead it was awful.

Even as I secretly looked forward to the end of cross-country and the subsequent requirement to stop running, I couldn't stop without some semblance of a fight. The Voice would not let me out of running that easily. I could not just quit. I needed someone to force me in order for it to be justifiable. Thus, the day after cross-country ended, I hit the road once again when I woke up. It was not a choice for me; I had to do it. My mother tried to talk to me, "I thought this was going to stop when cross country ended." Nope. It was my obsession, my life. For a week I continued to train with the team in a group we called Snow Cats. When I went to my weekly appointment with the nutritionist, she told me I had to stop running.

"Your weight is too low, Rae, don't you see that? You are in danger of having a heart attack or breaking bones. You can't lose anymore weight, and your body can no longer support the running." Her words managed to frighten some part of me that was deeply buried. I knew her words would haunt me, but this fear was not as powerful as the Voice.

I went home and told my mom the nutritionist was not helping me at all and I did not want to go anymore. I could not handle the pressure I felt when I went there. The suffocating room full of brochures and plastic pieces of food made me sick. It was suffocating both physically and mentally. It was someone trying to take control. I could not breathe when I walked in that room. I felt sick, and the experience went downhill from there as I watched her look at my food charts. She would say things like, "Maybe you could drink a little whole milk with this," or, "You need more than an apple for lunch." I would agree and tell her I would try to work on that while my mind was screaming "No!"

After I stopped going to my nutritionist, things got a little easier for a while. There were no more food records that I had to answer for at the end of the week, no more weighing myself and getting in trouble for my so-called accomplishments. I felt free again and like I had regained a bit of control. The feeling was good and scary all at the same time. I was able to revert back to my eating (or not eating) patterns, and no one was able to watch me. I had become the master of making excuses for not eating.

However, at the same time I was scared, because I was realizing the direction in which my control was taking me. The words of my counselor and nutritionist had made a little chink in my wall. There was a small part of me that cared if I died. It was like this little voice that battled in me for my life. Maybe it was the self I had never paid attention to. Of course, most of the time I ignored it. It wasn't right to listen to this little voice that was trying desperately to save my life. Nonetheless, it was difficult to have it nagging me, and the nutritionist just made this annoying little voice all the stronger. Refusing this voice was too much to bear with a nutritionist on my back. I was aware that I was not normal, that my obsession was just that, an obsession. Normal people did not think like me, and I was starving myself. I knew, but I could not make myself care. That kind of feeling was long gone. I could not make myself listen to my therapist and family: I did not want to hear them, and I pushed them away. I let their words wash over me. Instead, I remained devoted to the Voice. It was what kept me from gaining weight, from getting too tired despite my starvation. It said to me, *You are getting so strong. Don't go and ruin this by eating.* And I believed it.

V
Counseling

It was several months before I finally agreed to see a second therapist at my mother's insistence. I was still reluctant about the whole thing. While I had acknowledged that something was wrong, I still had a hard time believing it. I guess I was walking the tightrope of denial. Some days, when I was so tired and low it took all I had to walk through my day, I knew that I was in trouble. Yet, even then, I could usually convince myself I was okay. Given this, the first day I went to meet my counselor, I was not entirely sold on the idea that I needed to be there. To put it more honestly, I was not sure I really wanted to get better. I did not want another situation with someone breathing down my neck, and somehow I knew that this was exactly what I was signing up for.

I walked into the small waiting room with my mother. Chairs lined the walls and there was a pile of biking magazines in the corner. There was another young girl in the room and we glanced at each other, our eyes meeting briefly. She had a tube coming out of her nose and it was taped to her cheek. I would learn what this was later, but at the time, I was puzzled by it. We both wondered what the other was there for, knowing it was none of our business, yet recognizing it was probably for the same problem. After the initial glance, we carefully avoided looking at each other by concentrating on the ground or the blank, beige wall...anything really.

Then the counselor opened the door and said my name. He had thinning, light brown hair and an imposing frame. But it was his eyes that caught my attention. For many sessions to come I would see those piercing eyes that made me feel utterly exposed. Maybe it was their pale blue color that made them seem capable of seeing things no ordinary person was capable of seeing. I don't know what it was, but I rarely wanted to look into those eyes. They were too intense, too full of truth somehow. I mostly focused on the wall. The wall was safe—it never reacted, never expressed emotion. Maybe I was scared of what those eyes would tell me through their reactions.

I followed him into his office, watching his calm, fluid steps. He had such a powerful, quiet presence, and although I did not want to be there, I found myself intrigued by this man. He wore Birkenstocks and khakis. I later discovered he rode a motorcycle or bike to work. He said riding a bike made him feel more connected to the nature surrounding him. He said it was the best way to travel. Whatever he was, he seemed to have it all together. It was like he held all of life's wisdom. Yet he rarely shared any answers. He left me to find my own answers, which often left me frustrated and confused. I wanted to find the key that would let me out of my hell, and I believed he held it. That was why I was there. I wanted to be fixed, and yet at the same time, I did not want to change anything. I wanted to stay in my starved euphoria.

It is such a strange state, starvation. You are half dead, and yet somehow you walk around in a state of euphoria. That is what my therapist explained to my mother on my first visit. It was true. I was angry when he described the feelings I was having as a false sense of energy. It seemed as if he classified me as just another patient with another disease, and these were the symptoms. I hated that. I was different; I wasn't just another case. I didn't know what I was, but I was not that. I really didn't want to be seen as one case among many; every fiber of me detested the idea. Maybe it was because I so desperately needed someone to help me find myself and this made me feel even further removed. Why couldn't he see that?

He told me that anorexia was a coping mechanism. He said that it was a way to cope with stress, because it gave a person something else to concentrate on instead of the issue that was truly causing her conflict. Essentially, it was a way to distract myself. He also said that when a person felt out of control, anorexia served as a means to regain a sense of control. His ideas held some merit, but something did not ring entirely true to me. Something in his explanation did not fit my situation, but I could not tell what it was. Of course, I was not ready to accept most of what he said anyway. I felt like I was not stressed, that things were coming easy to me. I was first in my class and I ended as first runner on my team in cross-country. Everything seemed pretty under control to me.

I wanted to stand up to him. I felt the arguments rise in my throat and choke me, but I could not say the arguments out loud on that first visit. I could not argue with this man. I looked at his eyes; they were so clear, so confident. It was as if he were truth embodied. Were my eyes that clear? I knew they were not. They were clouded; they stared at walls for hours on end. My eyes took hours to read my homework because I couldn't put the words together anymore. I knew that deep down my therapist was telling me the truth, but every part of me wanted to argue.

The Voice was there inside my head screaming so loudly that I barely heard his words. No, that was not true. I heard his words loud and clear, but they had no effect, I did not let them touch me. They only made me feel angry and defiant. I was angry because he was breaking down my defenses, and every truth he told me made me angrier because it ruined the world I had worked so hard to build. It protected me, and he was taking it away, piece by painful piece. He never asked if he could, he just did. It seemed like so many people in my life took without asking, and it broke my heart to have this taken away. Even while my actions were slowly killing me, they were also serving a very important purpose. They were relieving my guilt and lessening my sense of failure. So I protected my world as best as I could. I held onto it tenaciously.

I did not listen to my counselor with my heart, only my ears. It seemed to be much like I had begun to live my life. My choices, my actions, were all made with my head, I never gave my heart or emotions consideration. I skimmed the surface. Nothing was deep, nothing was unsolvable...until him. Everything I had buried started to come out of hiding. I pushed my emotions back down because the feelings were too much; I could not understand them. I no longer spoke their language.

In many ways, our first session together seemed typical. I told him about myself. I am sure he heard all of the familiar characteristics that classify an "anorexic." I worked hard at school, I was a perfectionist, and I was highly disciplined and rigid in my daily schedule at that point. As I described my life to him, I knew the description fit perfectly into anorexic stereotypes and it killed me to think I was fitting into his classification system. I think I cried during the first session. I cannot remember. I cried so many times in his office. His office came to be filled with so much emotion for me. There were so many contradictory associations with that room: beautiful breakthroughs and awful moments of loneliness and confusion.

Against two walls were big, dark green leather couches. In the corner was his desk where he sat. He would lean back in his chair with his clipboard and take notes as I talked. I always spent lots of time inspecting and asking about the photographs on his walls. They were usually pictures of scenery, and there was always a story behind each one. I made a habit of turning to those photos when I did not want to talk about myself. He would usually humor me and answer my questions, although I am sure he understood my intentions. He was so quiet. He rarely said much, yet when he did, his words usually stuck with me. They haunted me.

One such conversation with my counselor went something like this:

Counselor: "How's school going?" (This was a typical opening question.)

Me: "Oh, good. Actually, it's pretty busy and stressful right now. You know, things are crazy and classes are busy, and you get anxious." (This was a typical answer.)

Counselor: "Who's anxious?" (Huh? Not typical.)

Me: "Me?"

Counselor: "Oh!" [feign surprise], "You're anxious."

Me: "Uh, yes."

Counselor: "So you would say, *I'm* anxious."

I would look at him confused when this sort of exchange initially began. Slowly, I figured out what he wanted me to say and I would repeat, "Yes, *I'm* anxious."

He would nod, and I would go on somewhat confused as to what he was getting at, but eventually I caught on. His points were always subtle like that. Finally one day, in utter exasperation, I asked what the hell he meant by acting all confused about who I was talking about when it was quite obvious I was talking about myself.

He replied, "Well, you always speak in second person. You say *you* when you're talking about your feelings, like you're not yourself."

I realized how removed from myself I was. I referred to myself in the second person. I had become an outside observer of myself. Who did I live in? Where was I? I never realized how disconnected I was until I realized I had to practice saying "I" when I talked about myself. The disconnection was essential for the critical abuse to which I subjected myself.

In a lot of ways, I lived for everyone else, the classic people pleaser. In order to be a successful people pleaser, it is important to deny one's separate identity, which possesses needs and desires of its own. I made sure I knew what others expected of me, and that was what I did. I was a people pleaser to the point of losing myself in others' expectations of me. I was a product of what others wanted. I operated this way not because I particularly liked it, but because it came easy to me. Pleasing people was how I got by without conflict, without anxiety, and without fear of losing someone's affection or positive regard. How can a person have conflict with someone when they are everything that person wants them to be? I had no voice of my own to tell them what I wanted. I was not entirely sure that wanting things for myself was even okay. It felt selfish. What would I even want? And, more important, who would be hurt or walk away from me because of my selfish pursuits? On some level, this way of behaving always made me feel like I was an observer of myself. How could I own anything I did? I was not my own, I was everyone else's.

I remember one therapy session very distinctly, because it was the day I came to the realization that I had no ability to assert myself and was uncomfortable with my own voice. I was sitting in my counselor's office and we were both silently staring. Me, staring at the wall wondering what to say. Him, staring at me waiting...just waiting. That godawful waiting. I sighed quietly, unaware of my action and the fact that he was watching me so intently. He sighed in response, but much more loudly, in such a way that it caused me to look at him, surprised. When I met his eyes, he challenged me with another loud sigh, then said, "You do it."

"Do what?" I asked him, "sigh loudly?"

"Yes."

I looked at him as if he were out of his mind. I thought it was stupid, what he was asking me to do. I felt silly, but I tried to sigh anyway. Lord knows, I tried. It was such a dumb challenge and seemingly an easy one. I was always ready for a chance to prove to everyone that I was fine, and somehow it felt like this challenge was not just any old challenge. For some reason I could sense that he knew I would not be able to sigh like that, and in not being able to do it, I would have to admit how much I really did need help. So I tried. Yet, whenever the moment came to forcibly pass sound out of my mouth with my sigh, I simply could not do it. Several times I attempted to meet his challenge while he watched me serenely as I began to panic. I remember looking at him, defeat in me, wondering why. Why could I not be loud? I was scared of being loud. I felt a bit frantic. I didn't say it out loud, of course, but my thoughts were racing. Why am I so scared to be heard? To let my voice rise above more than just a quiet, background sound? To share my thoughts, or something as simple as a sigh? What haunts me? What holds me back? Is it the possibility of ridicule? laughter? that maybe I won't be taken seriously? What if I am not the person they think I am?

It was an unnerving moment for me. I thought about it a great deal. I went home and wrote about it. It was difficult to directly experience how disempowered I felt, and how I had made myself so insignificant that I couldn't even sigh loudly in a room with another person.

VI
Mind versus Body

My mind was everything. My body was simply my tool, my disappointment, my faulty wrapper. I never thought of my body and mind as one; I never saw my body as part of me. I once heard anorexia described as the ultimate betrayal of the body. This is true. Anorexia denies the body its main source of survival–food. Everything the body tells a person falls on deaf ears if the person is anorexic. The body is something to be denied. Strangely, a person does not see her body as part of her "self." Anorexia could not only be described as the ultimate betrayal of the body, but also as the ultimate betrayal of the self and the metaphorical expression of the self, simultaneously.

The very roots of the first eating disorders–though they were not called disorders initially–can be traced back to the separation of body and mind. From religious aesthetics that achieved ultimate godly devotion by starvation and separation from the material world to St. Liberata, a princess who starved herself to gain freedom from her arranged marriage, self-induced starvation has always carried with it a deranged sort of strength and pride. Religious ascetics were some of the first documented people who intentionally starved themselves to death. It was their goal to reach the spiritual realm, and in order to do this, they had to escape the "earthly" hindrance of their bodies. By taking their lives, by starving themselves to death, they demonstrated the highest reverence to God possible. Ascetics saw humans as evil, as filthy. The only way to be close to God was to transcend your humanity, the very thing that made you unworthy.

During the course of my anorexia, I distinctly remember feeling pride in my strength as I declined meals while everyone else *had* to eat due to hunger. I felt my starvation somehow made me separate from the human condition. Self-starvation is a means of escape, whereby a person finds a false sense of liberation. This ambivalent attitude remains in popular culture. Eating disorders have become just that, *disorders*, illnesses, and yet, they are still revered. Frequently, it is not healthy women who are seen as famous, successful, and beautiful; instead, it is women who could be classified as anorexic. This sends many girls the wrong message: in order to be successful, you must be thin.

Many regard eating disorders with a certain amount of disgust. Why would a person starve herself to death? Why would she be so damn set on it when you ask her to stop? Many people with anorexia are similar to ascetics in that they, on some level, see themselves at their core as bad. They are sensitive, especially when it comes to how they affect others, and inevitably they make mistakes, because we all do. However, the hurt they inflict cuts them to the core, and they are disgusted with themselves. They expect perfection and forget that they are human. In fact, they try desperately to convince themselves that they can somehow escape their humanity. Thus, they detach from the very thing that makes them human, their physical form. They become machine-like, because this is their only hope. I know that the times I was happiest with myself were the times when I felt mechanical. When I didn't need food, when I didn't feel. I felt hope—that I wouldn't be a failure, that I was worthy of people's love. But the only way to do this was to completely detach from my body.

My counselor subtly showed me how out of touch I was with my body. I would be attempting to tell him my thoughts on some subject, and he would interject with a question like, "How does your body feel right now?" I would be utterly confused and at a loss as to how my body felt. So he would teach me how to pay attention to what my body was telling me. He would ask, "Do you feel tense, and where?" Initially, he would have to answer his questions for me. I was so out of touch that an observer could tell what my body was feeling better than I could. I was accustomed to ignoring what it told me.

He would say, "I see your shoulders tensing up as you think. You are holding your breath. Relax your shoulders, take a breath." As soon as he told me these things, I felt the tenseness and my breath would come out in a big exhale.

He never spelled anything out for me, and because he said so little, his few words were valuable. I often hated this. I longed for him to fill the silences with words, any words. I just wanted noise. I did not want the responsibility of having to talk; it took too much energy to think, and inevitably feelings would come. Feelings were dangerous, especially because many of the feelings I was protecting myself from were negative. One word best sums up my emotions: despair. Facing these horrible feelings took time and energy, and I did not have any of that to spare. Many times I would simply sit in that office staring at the wall, hating the fact that I hated the silence more than anything and knowing that I would eventually talk out of sheer desperation. I would look for safe things to talk about. Safe, meaning inconsequential. I talked about how busy I was, how hard practice was, but he always found a way to make the subject more than superficial.

Without these weekly appointments with my counselor, I could convince myself that I was empty. Emptiness. It was to be endured, suffered through, and yet embraced at the same time. It sat upon my shoulders. It suffocated me sometimes. Like sap, the more I tried to rid myself of the feeling, the stickier it became. Emptiness clung to my entire being. It made me dead in many ways. I wanted to be dead inside. I did not want to feel the pressure to succeed. I did not want to feel the bothersome loneliness that seemed to plague me. I did not want to feel the pain of failing those that loved me. Emptiness was actually a relief. It allowed me to focus on survival.

As my junior year progressed that fall, I did not feel distracted by worries, and I became the most productive I have ever been. I ran twice a day, I did my homework, I volunteered at a nearby vet clinic in the evenings... produce, perform, just do. But then I would have to go to therapy, to the doctor, and to the nutritionist. This was the cost of the emptiness that I strove for and that I hated all at the same time. As the world I had built was slowly deconstructed before my eyes, I began to realize how much of myself I had lost, killed, and forgotten.

Every day I would tell myself, *Tomorrow things will get easier, things will get better. Tomorrow you'll do it right, Rae.* Every tomorrow became a today, and every today brought another letdown, and every letdown brought me closer to my reality, to my fear. I was so scared of a life full of letdowns, pain, and disappointment. A life full of lost control, lost motivation, lost self-worth, and lost self-confidence. Every day I felt closer to my fear and further from my goal. It was painful to look in the mirror; I hated to see myself. I no longer sought out my friends because my self-consciousness had become intolerable. Getting dressed almost brought me to tears. I felt so fat. People would try to normalize these feelings for me, saying, "It's okay, everyone feels depressed sometimes, what you are feeling is normal." But this was not normal: my various appointments were slowly destroying *this* and it was not normal.

I felt so afraid that there was no way to get away from it. I wanted so badly to talk about how confused, devastated, and completely obsessed I was, but it was all locked up somewhere. When I tried to talk about it, it was like groping in the dark for a mysterious object and never knowing if I had found it or not because I couldn't feel it. I was slowly coming to realize that for all the lightness and the weird sense of strength that I felt, I was actually trapped, and I was so sick of it. But even as I sensed this, I didn't know how to get it out of myself. I felt so far away from anything, from everything. Sometimes I thought I had lost myself and there was no coming back.

I desperately needed to feel normal again. I needed to get anorexia out of me before it became me, but everything felt hazy, and conviction turned to uncertainty in a matter of moments. I felt so restless: waiting, tossing, turning, aching for something more than what I had become. I never felt relief. My nightmare was constant and I was afraid it would never end. I couldn't bring myself to tell anyone my fears because they were an embarrassment to me. I wished I could hide the physicality that revealed my problems; I wished they couldn't see. I felt so weak and vulnerable. I was destroying myself.

I'm sure it scared everyone to watch anorexia take me over. I think they tried to control their fears by putting anorexia into a nice little package. They came up with answers that seemed to fit, which were mostly transient issues that arise during adolescence and would pass as I grew up. I think it helped take away the permanence that anorexia can have in a person's life, whether through death or transformation into a living ghost of a person. I hated this. I wanted to say to them, *I am not a study; I am not a blueprint; I am not a puzzle you can take apart and put together.*

VII
Routine

Can you go too deep? Can you travel the depths of your mind so far you lose all awareness of what's real? Where nothing touches you anymore; no one can reach you. Where your biggest fear becomes yourself. Can you isolate yourself so totally that you no longer realize you're lonely? And those you love become obstacles and chores, and you can't touch them; you no longer see them, because all you can see is yourself. They won't save you because they can't. And why is it on the journey back, you realize you are more alone than you have ever been, and you are so afraid sometimes you can't breathe? Yet you keep going...keep climbing, keep falling...you just keep going.

-Journal Entry, November 1998

Cross-country ended and the winter of my junior year set in. I fell further and further into myself, into "the Voice." I fell into a haunting world that was strangely disconnected from everything. My days slowly became more tiring. Without cross-country and running, I worried more and more about gaining weight, so I cut back on food as much as I could. I would walk through the halls after lunch, going to each class and trying hard to focus, but I was so cold. I never warmed up. I started wearing layers; sometimes I wore three shirts. Short sleeves were out of the question. First because I was too cold, second because my arms had become skeletal and people noticed. I did not want anyone to notice; I wanted to disappear.

I would go home after school, build a fire as quickly as I could, and stand in front of it for most of the night. I stood there and stared at the wall, just stared. I remember feeling nothing except the warmth of the fire. I did my homework by the fire. At eleven o' clock every night, I went to bed. In bed I would plan what I was gong to eat the next day and come up with punishments if I did not stick to the set meals. Before I had to stop running, these punishments would be running an extra mile, but now they became skimping on a meal later that day or not letting myself eat something I liked to eat. I would still try to devise ways to work in exercise. Sometimes I would walk after school before my mom came home. If I had enough courage and energy, I would run. Isolation set in. I started to pull away from friends and spent very little time with them outside of school. Crushes that I had had faded, and I removed them from my mind. My mom would ask me about boys I used to talk about. I would shake my head and say I did not really like them anymore. I was over them. That was the end of the conversation.

I was so buried in my own head that I did not notice my mother's pain. I later found out that she was on Paxil, an anti-anxiety drug. She would rush home from work to make dinner in hopes that I would eat. Of course, by this point I was a master of lies and excuses. "I ate after school and I'm not hungry." Or, "I can't eat pasta, it makes my stomach hurt." And my favorite, "Mom, I'm sorry I can't eat after seven o' clock, it sits in my stomach all night and makes me feel sick in the morning." This lie was the best because it was often very difficult to get dinner on the table before seven. My mom learned to make soups and salads, as these were the only things I really ate without much protest.

My mom was the holder of all of the emotion I pushed down in myself. She took it on. All through cross-country season, she skipped work for every race. I never told her how badly I needed her there, but she must have known, because she never missed and was rarely late, a true feat for my mom. It became a tradition for me to find her before every race and hug her tightly while I buried my head in her shoulder and sobbed, hidden from the view of my teammates. I needed this to relieve the intense anxiety I felt before each race. As the season went on I gradually grew more and more apprehensive. I never trusted that I would be able to finish the race. It was such a daunting task to run three miles as fast as I could. My emotions were never as heightened as they were before a race. My mom would hug me until the tears passed, reassuring me that whatever happened, it would be okay. It must have torn her up to cheer me on each race as she watched me waste away. She would promise to get me treats after the race, whatever I wanted, and often the treat would become my mantra as I ran. Yet, after finishing, I never wanted the treat, or I would nibble at something to make my mom feel better.

After cross-country ended, and as I continued my appointments with my therapist, my eyes began to see my mom again. I believe she was the first person I really saw again and cared about. Sometimes she would come to my sessions with me. She was always so strong. She would ask questions and try to understand. She would talk to my counselor while I sat beside her and listened to the conversation. One day she cried. I had seen her cry before, but this time I knew she was crying because of me. She was sitting across the room from me and she looked at me with tears in her eyes, pleading with me to listen. For a minute my mortality became very real to me. It was clear for a brief moment what I was doing. I cried with her. I felt so bad for putting her through this. But the moment of clarity passed, the Voice stepped in, and my resolve to take care of myself faded just as quickly as it had come.

A few times we had family meetings with my therapist. Once, we went around the room and each person told me how he or she felt watching me starve myself. I remember what my older brother said, and I remember what my seven-year-old sister did. My brother, who was away at college during this time, looked at me. Then he looked at my therapist and said, "Every time I see her, there is less of her. Not just physically, but it's like the person within the body is dying." His face was tense, holding back his emotions. I was very familiar with this face. My little sister hid behind my mother, too shy to say anything. But later, she wrote me a letter in her beautiful second-grade handwriting. She said it made her so sad to see me be sad and that she prayed for me while she watched me dance in our living room. I often danced all alone in our big living room. In the dark, when I was sad, I would dance. I never knew she watched; that is how oblivious I was.

Every human has a basic instinct to survive. How could someone deliberately starve herself to death? For me, it was a matter of strength, perfection, and control. A person cannot afford to feel if she wants control and perfection. A person cannot afford to be human because humans are not in control, and humans are not that strong, at least not by themselves. So, in an attempt to be in control, I denied my feelings by holding them inside. The feelings do not go away though. Instead, I got too full and somehow I had to make room for more, because the feelings kept coming. I swallowed so many negative feelings, the doubts, the shame, and the sadness. I internalized all of this, but the feelings came out in the Voice. The anger, the disappointment, all of it was somehow turned on myself. It was not okay to feel these things towards others, so I found a way to put it on myself.

It's like a messy room you neglect too long. For a while, it's much easier to pick through the mess than to deal with it. But the buildup inevitably gets too high and you can no longer ignore it. When I finally faced my mess, it had become so large that I was overwhelmed. I didn't know where to begin. I looked for distractions from this painful situation, but when there were none, I focused on food and size. I knew on some level that I needed to pay attention to myself. It was my soul that needed nurturing, not my body that needed abuse.

I didn't know where to begin. I would ask myself, *What do I feel? What is bothering me?* But my responses were limited to how much I had eaten or how disgusted I felt about my body. I was constantly frustrated by these feelings, and I couldn't seem to get past them. There were occasions when I got upset and someone would ask me how I felt about it. I always found it very difficult to answer them. It seemed too hard to decipher my feelings. They were a mystery even to me. Maybe I knew vaguely how I felt, but I never wanted to go further than that. So instead, I focused on food or exercise, and this left me more confused than when I had begun.

I made room in my stomach for the feelings I couldn't deal with. The less food I ate, the more room I had to swallow my feelings. It became easier to push the feelings down. I felt strong as I developed the ability to not eat and to deny my feelings. I thought that not eating (restricting) made me stronger. It was not really strength; rather it was sinking further into a starved, delirious state. I was winning at the game I had set up for myself. I was driven to brutally discipline myself.

I started seeing another nutritionist that my therapist recommended. They worked together closely. I liked her better than the first. She was more reasonable in pushing me to eat, and she at least made the effort to identify with me. She knew about eating disorders and understood them in a way that comes with years of experience. I took comfort in this. She was tiny, with beautiful, lively eyes. Sometimes I imagined that just by looking into her eyes, she would give mine a little life. She worked with my therapist and my doctor. They would have team meetings. My life had become a blur of appointments. My extracurricular activities slowly became my appointments. I liked my nutritionist, and eventually she became a counselor, a friend, and a mother to me in her own way. However, when she first came into my life, she was yet another person looking over my shoulder, and I was wary. There were so many people watching my every move. They knew my thoughts, my weight, and what I ate every day. I had to work hard to hide as much as I could.

Sometimes I said I ate more than I did, and often I did not say what I was feeling. Sometimes I wore three shirts when I got weighed. That was my protection, my control. I still had something over them. They could not know everything, and they never would. Of course, she could see my three shirts, and my weight reflected the truth of my food records. That did not cross my mind at the time. I was desperate to hang onto my way of life, to my weight. It was all I had.

VIII
Balloons

One day, the inevitable violation of my control came. I was at one of my regular appointments with my therapist, and my mother had come into the room with us. He was telling my mom that we could not let my weight drop below a certain point, because that was when a person's mind truly became unable to think correctly and to reason. He said my weight was hovering dangerously close to this point, given my frame and build. He said it would be much harder to bring me back if my weight dropped below this certain point. I sat there listening, not caring much. I had been hovering at my current weight for a couple months and to me it still seemed just a bit heavy, but no one was putting pressure on me as long as I did not lose too much too fast. Then I was snapped to attention by his next statement.

"We could put her on a feeding tube. I have done that with other patients, and it seems to be the most successful way to recovery."

I imagined being filled with air like a balloon, except the air was an incessant stream of calories being poured down my throat. I saw by body growing unstoppably, filling up just like the balloon. My insides flopped and churned at the very thought of it. I started to plead with him. I told him I did not want to gain weight back that way, I wanted to taste my food. I desperately wanted to taste my food, and I meant it. I really did. I wanted one more chance. I implored him for one last chance. He granted me that and set an ultimatum. He told me that for the next three weeks weight needed to go up steadily—meaning at least a pound every week or two—otherwise, I would go on a feeding tube. Ah, safe for another three weeks. It seemed like a long time since I rarely thought past my next meal. Three weeks was years away. I relaxed.

During the following weeks I would get worried every now and then, but for the most part I ignored his ultimatum. It seemed too far away, and I was too set in my patterns. I did not even try half-heartedly. In fact, I managed to lose more weight. Looking back, my therapist's theory had rung true. I was not going to take the initiative to gain weight. I had stopped battling the Voice a long time ago. I was sick and tired of being where I was, but there wasn't an ounce of fight left in me. I had surrendered to the abuse running through my head and had succumbed to each stupid limit that I set for myself. The only fight I had now was how I could eat less and still get through my days. I wasn't striving for survival anymore. My family saw this, and they did the only thing they knew to do.

Time passes whether you acknowledge it or not, and three weeks came and went. The moment came despite my denial. One Sunday night, as my dad was getting ready to go back to his job two hours away, he broke the news to me. He walked up to me while I was warming myself by the heater in our kitchen and he hugged me. Then he said, "I'm sorry. I am taking the decision out of your hands. I'll be back on Thursday. You have an appointment at Sacred Heart Hospital to get a feeding tube put in. You need to make arrangements with your teachers at school." He said this in his warmest, gentlest voice, but it carried authority. There was no room for discussion about his decision.

I went limp; I melted into his hug. I didn't have the energy to be angry or to question or to fight his decision. All of my life, whatever my dad said had been law. That was how it was. This was no different.

There was no question that I would be out of school while I had the feeding tube. They wanted me to stay home and rest, and I could not imagine answering questions. I did not want to be the school freak; I already felt crazy. I knew my peers would be less than understanding or tactful about the subject. I hadn't ever talked to anyone about this. None of my friends knew what was happening and neither did my coaches or teachers.

That Monday, I went to school early and mechanically went through the steps. My parents let me make all of the arrangements myself. I guess it made me face what was happening. First, I went to the counseling office where I told the junior class counselor that I would not be in school for the next semester. She told me she could arrange for a tutor to bring my schoolwork to me so that I wouldn't get behind. She was kind and compassionate about the whole situation. I had to tell her why, and she listened quietly. I had never had to say to anyone that I was struggling with anorexia. Never had those words passed my lips, and suddenly, on this day, they had to. It was the hardest thing I had ever said, and the emotion that followed in the wake of the words left me feeling defeated and ashamed.

I told all of my teachers, but telling the first teacher was the worst. I went to my AP history classroom before school started. I had grown close to my teacher, and I respected him a lot. It had become my habit to go to his classroom early several days a week and study before classes began. I walked up to his desk. He asked what was up, and the words flowed out of my mouth before I could stop myself. "I won't be at school next semester, and there's going to be a tutor who can take my work to me, if that's okay with you. I won't be here because...I'm--I'm struggling a bit with anorexia and I have to go on a feeding tube." I tripped over the last words. I didn't know how to say them, and I was too scared to look at his face because I was sure his reaction would be disgust. I looked down as I said "anorexia;" I couldn't bear it.

As I studied the ground, I heard him say, "I know, Rae. I have been wondering if you were getting help; I have been watching you this semester. Of course we can work something out with your schoolwork, don't worry about it. You don't need to drop the class. You just get yourself better, okay?" Tears stung my eyes. It was so embarrassing to tell him. I felt so much shame, and suddenly I knew my problem must have been so apparent. This had never occurred to me. I had never expected this sort of kindness and acceptance, and it touched me even as I was drowning in embarrassment.

I was in a fog while telling my other teachers. I didn't tell most of my friends. I couldn't. I told only one. I had run with her that year, and she was in my AP Biology class. I remember sitting in the hall with her as I told her and it was awful. She hugged me. She told me everything was going to be okay. I sat in the hallway for the whole period with her. Telling people took the perfection out of it. Suddenly, I was not strong, I was ill. I was crazy. I was mentally unstable and sick. When no one knew, when it was my secret, the mystery made it seem different. I didn't know telling people would change it like that. It was disappointing and disgusting to me.

It was January 24th, two days before my seventeenth birthday and the week after semester finals. I went to my favorite bakery with my parents and my sister before going to the hospital. As usual, I picked at my food. I remember looking at my reflection in the glass, wondering where this day would take me. I studied my profile in the reflection and saw that from the side, I was nearly nonexistent. I made myself remember that picture—my baggy sweatshirt, my baggy jeans, and my tennis shoes that looked bulky at the end of my thin legs. I was in a daze. I hugged my sister in front of the hospital and someone gave me a Winnie the Pooh balloon. I thought, *a balloon, a fucking balloon. Like I'm going to the dentist or something.* To this day, every time I happen to drive by that place I am transported back to that moment like it was yesterday. As we sat in the waiting room, I looked at magazines, the coffee machines, my parents; I did not say anything.

A nurse walked into the waiting room and called my name. She led me into a room where I lay down on a cold metal table with an x-ray coat over me. I could not tell whether it was the lead coat or me that made me feel so crushed. I could not breathe as I lay down on that table. I was letting go of my anorexia. I was not ready; I would never be ready. I could not escape, I could not move. I went through the motions, unthinking, unfeeling, like I did everything else in my life. I sniffed the numbing gel up my nose until I could feel it running down the back of my throat. I watched the nurse put the tube up my nose, and I felt it glide down the back of my throat into my stomach. I watched the x-ray screen as she placed the end of the tube in my intestine. She taped the other end to my cheek and I sat up. I walked mechanically down the hall, my spirit gone. When I saw my father in the waiting room, it hit me. Tears came, panic began, and as I felt the hot warmth of my tears, I knew something had given way in me. I felt broken, a sad shadow of what I had been. The tube made me see how far away I was from the person I used to know as myself.

I didn't yet know it, but the worst was still to come. From the hospital we went to an office to pick up the formula I would "feed" myself and to get instructions on how to use my feeding tube. When I walked into the office I was shocked to see a familiar face. The lady who would be instructing me on how to use the tube was the mom of a friend from cross-country. Her eyes widened when she saw me, and I hung my head in shame and embarrassment. She rushed to inform me about the privacy practices and to assure me that she would not tell my friend what she knew. Then we left the subject alone.

Four hours later, I left with IV bags, a stand, and formula running at 55 cc's through my tube into me. I didn't know how much 55 cc's was, but it sounded and felt like a lot. This was the worst part. Every part of me knew what was happening, and like an addict, I started shaking. I was tense and thought I was going to lose it. For me, this was the ultimate relinquishment of control, and control was all I had left along with my fear—my fear of gaining weight, which was inevitable now. Every night at eight o' clock I would have to fill an IV bag with four cans of formula—each can providing 250 calories—then connect it to my feeding tube and start the pump.

IX
Taking home the Tube

Slithering down my throat,
burrowing a single hole in my wall.
Filling my nose, my ears, flooding my senses.
I must remember why; I must stay calm.
Oh, but the screaming is starting inside,
and the straining is overtaking my body.
Don't crumble the wall.
Please don't ruin it all.
It's snaking through my stomach,
penetrating my soul.
And someday it will make me better.
I must remember why; I must stay calm.
I feel the screaming rise.
It flows out of my eyes.
The tears are starting to fall,
washing over pieces of my wall.
And suddenly I can't remember why.
I don't want to remember why.

-Journal Entry, January 24, 1999

I could not handle it that first night. I lay on the floor moaning, crying, and screaming, until my father called the nurse and she told him I could turn the rate down to 50 cc's. That night, I lost all control. Every time I heard the pump, I thought I would go crazy.

My shrunken stomach felt like it would pop. And then, to punish myself further, I began to eat. I found a way to make feeding myself a punishment. I ate ice cream, chips, crackers...so many foods I hadn't let myself eat for so long. I ate until my stomach churned and ached and then I cried tears of frustration, shame, and disgust. I wanted to die rather than to live with the feelings I was experiencing. Yet, even then there was a tiny voice that said, "Live, Rae." Out of pure desperation, I began to write. Any activity that took my attention away from the pump was welcome.

I could hear the steady tick of the pump sitting beside me, feel the tube running across my cheek, up my nose, and register the irritating pain in my throat every time I swallowed. As I sat there listening to the pump, I knew what it was doing and every part of my mind was fighting it, but my body was so exhausted it wouldn't side with my mind. Yet I couldn't fully resign myself to it.

That day, I made a choice by not fighting my father's choice. I knew it could very well be the only thing that would break the pattern. But the enticing thought of not breaking the pattern beckoned to me—it was easier to go downhill. Something stopped me though. I knew there was nothing waiting for me down there except more agony like this. So I started to climb, and the first step felt excruciating. I hoped some parts of the journey back would be beautiful and breathtaking, but I couldn't know for sure.

I was scared. Half of me was relieved that I wouldn't have to do all the work myself, but the other half was scared to death and holding back. I kept thinking, *I can't do this, I won't.* But I was. I felt so mad at everyone. I felt like they had taken something away from me. WHY? The Voice told me it was pointless, unnecessary to have this tube. *I was fine. I felt fine.* In fact, I was exhausted. I was tired of counting calories, of having cold hands, of feeling dizzy and tired. I was tired of barely getting through my days and considering a piece of pizza a guilty feast. I was tired of crying after dinner, of staring at walls, of fighting with myself every time I wanted to eat. I wanted to be NORMAL!

The fear become more real with every second that passed. *How will I ever face myself if I weigh 120 pounds? How can I let myself gain that much weight? How could I possibly love myself like that?*

The tube was an unwanted intruder. That night, alone in my room, I turned the rate down to 35 cc's, and then I cried. I cried for all that I had lost and mourned every calorie dripping into my body. I cried like I hadn't cried for so long, and I prayed to a God I was not really sure of. I felt like a small child who looks up to find her mother gone from her side. She looks frantically around as the fear wells up in her and the emotion spills out, uncontrollable. She reaches for anything familiar, anything that will provide comfort. I needed someone to take my hand so badly, and no one could. God felt like my last desperate reach for company in this hell. I was scared, I was confused, and I was ashamed. I saw the seriousness now. Tomorrow I would not go to school, and if I never learned to eat, someday, much before my time, I was going to die. But I was petrified by the thought of this tube pumping calories into me and gaining weight. My head spun with so many contradictory fears. I felt paralyzed, unable to move or think in any consistent direction. I learned how alone I was that night. No one, not even a feeding tube, could heal me. I would have to depend solely on myself.

Every night I had to raise the rate of my pump by 5 cc's an hour, and it took every ounce of my courage to deal with the full feeling in my stomach. I eventually got to a point where my stomach and mind could handle 55 cc's an hour, but the thought of going past that scared me to death. It was the same with eating. I wanted to taste my food; I wanted to eat. I told myself I was going to eat, but at the end of the day, somehow I felt good if I had eaten only a muffin and some dried fruit.

A wall loomed in front of me, and at times I wanted to see what was on the other side. But other times—most times—I was used to what I knew, and something new sounded scary, too scary. I approached the wall, touched it, felt it, and maybe pushed against it a little. Then I got scared and backed away. As I distanced myself, I felt myself falling away, like part of me was connected to it. But I also found a feeling that comforted me. It said, *It's okay Rae, you feel good, stay here.* I knew I couldn't though. The wall beckoned to me at times and repelled me when I got too close. The wall represented my fear, and I knew it was holding me back from life.

Many mornings I would set my alarm so that I could get up before my mother and dump out some of the formula that was left in the bag. Every time I did this, I knew I was sabotaging myself, like a student cheating on a test. I was only hurting myself, but the battle was constantly waging in my mind, and sometimes it was too much to bear. The feeding tube was horribly invasive at times, yet other times it was a relief. It took care of me and carried some of the burden for me. The feeding tube pulled me into the fray of my chaos. It was the mother holding my hand, dragging me into the classroom on the first day of school. I do not know how long it would have taken me to start eating again without it, or if I ever would have.

X
Culture

Claws, I see claws ensnaring and scraping through my mind. Nowhere am I safe. There is no place to hide, my refuge has become occupied with a heart taker. An evil wager must be won before I can return to my one refuge. My hiding place is no longer safe. And I'm alone in the dark, searching desperately for the light. Why must my fight be fought on my own? There's no place to rest. What if I fail this test? Oh, please light, come shine on me. Help set me free; I am caught in my nightmare, and the claws have me in their snare.

-Journal Entry, March 1999

When I became aware of how alone I was in making my recovery happen, I experienced a deep fear. It kept me up at night. I listened to that damn pump and with each rhythmic, mechanical beat, my breath caught in my throat and I thought I would not be able to take another. Yet, when I once again breathed in air, I was not flooded with relief—instead another kind of dread filled me. I knew that I was just at the beginning of the journey, and I had no confidence that I alone could bring myself out of this dark place.

As I was trying to get better, I wanted reassurance that once it was gone, it would never come back, and that one day I wouldn't even remember it. Instead, the assurance I got was that a recovered anorexic is like a recovered alcoholic. It sticks with you because it's a coping mechanism, a way of controlling one's life when nothing else works. It is dangerous in that even after recovery, it can sneak up on you when you think you are in the clear. However, if you remain aware, it is possible to catch the anorexic thoughts and tell them "no."

The thought of this kind of life was not appealing. I often entertained the idea of relapsing and letting myself be thrown back into the pit of a hopeless anorexic. It was hard to understand how recovery would be much better than living as I was. I didn't want to relapse, and I didn't want anorexia once I was recovered. I wanted to thrive, not just survive. I had to disregard any notion that this wasn't possible.

A crucial part of making sure I would not relapse was that I had to go beneath the surface and find out what I was trying to cope with. I had to become more aware of what I was trying to numb in myself. In my search, I often felt very alone. I realized that there were few people who understood the complexities of anorexia and what it says metaphorically. For each individual it may be a different statement, but all the same, it is crucial to one's survival and happiness. To the onlooker, it makes no sense to starve oneself, and in an attempt to find something to blame, many people point to our culture's focus on beauty and its preoccupation with being thin as the main culprit. In the mainstream, anorexia is often understood as vain adolescents or adults trying to look attractive.

This perspective does not completely resonate with my experience. What my body looked like was a superficial covering to the deeper purpose and expression behind my anorexia. There was a great deal of pain behind what I was doing, not vanity. When I was upset because I ate too much or because I felt too full and fear overtook me, it was not about how I looked. Anorexia is ugly. Starvation is not pretty to watch. The obsession, for me, was about far more than beauty. My obsession—the thing that ate at me day and night—was not understood. It was frustrating.

There were certainly factors in American culture that played a role for me, but they were more complex than an explanation that focused on vanity as the main contributor. When I imagine our cultural attitude personified, I see a highly self-conscious person who is preoccupied with being independent (which falsely means never needing anyone) but inside she is dying of loneliness. This person is cut off from her feelings, because in order to feel the most difficult feelings, she usually needs someone to be with her. There is no one, because in her skewed definition of independent she believes that she cannot ask for someone to be there. She hopes to be beautiful because of what it symbolizes. A beautiful body symbolizes success, which leads to love, which results in never having to ask someone to be there because people will flock to you and pay attention. These are some of the cultural characteristics that caused difficulty for me: superficially status driven, hyper-individualism, and uncomfortable with almost all negative emotions.

I struggle with hopeless moments of self loathing. I struggle with letting my emotions be felt and expressed. I have a hard time believing that people will not judge and walk away from me on account of the slightest flaw. These are the problems I face when I cannot get over how much I ate or how little I exercised. Western culture has fed this inability to unconditionally accept oneself in its incessant emphasis on production, "success," and busyness. No one can just "be" anymore and be okay with that. No one can exist without swimming upstream, no one is allowed to flow, to be alive and to be grateful and appreciative of this in and of itself. Instead, at age five, we are sent to school. We have a fulltime job even as children. We produce, we perform, and we are nothing if we have nothing to show. It is a rat race, a madness, a frenzy. We are only free if we somehow manage to escape the rat race, which rarely happens.

One misconception that I had was that there was a finish line, a race I had to win. But, there is no finish line, and no one wins the race. The race is never ending, and many people become imprisoned in this way of life. A mystic I read once asked, "Why are you racing? What are you racing for? Death?" The faster you race the sooner death comes. I can no longer see the merit in racing so fast, but I am seduced by the race nonetheless, and while in the throes of anorexia, I believe my soul was rebelling against the life I thought I had to live. Instead of checking out of the race, I threw myself into it, and my body became an outward expression of the broken spirit with which I lived. Anorexia had so much control over me that the fight was no longer about denial but about realizing that I had become a puppet to my mind and I did not know how to take control of my thoughts anymore.

XI
Isolation

I had the feeding tube for about five months. I missed the second half of my junior year in high school. It was spent by the fireplace in our living room with schoolwork from my tutor surrounding me. The schoolwork was my one connection to reality outside of my house and my mind. I worked diligently every day; it was the only thing that transported me out of my thoughts. Once a week the tutor came to my house with all of my work, and I would send all of my completed assignments back to school with her. The memory is still too vivid. It seems like time stopped, or passed in slow motion, and I am able to document every detail in my memory. I can feel the heat at my back from the fireplace, the tube taped to my cheek, the silence, the stillness. I can see the stacks of work separated by subject. I hated and loved being alone. I had no energy for people and yet there were times I craved company. The quiet was deafening at times, but the thought of seeing friends exhausted me, because I knew I would have to put on a show for them. I would have to smile at the right times, I would have to be happy to see them, and all the while I would be dying inside.

I'm walking on thin ice, trying to convince everyone watching that it really is safe, that I'm not scared. But the truth is I'm scared to death, and whether or not they see it, the ice is thin. And what lies beneath is a mystery, a mystery I'm not sure I want to solve. It's dark, it's complex and so incomprehensible. Maybe it's all just dead. The cliche goes, "You are what you eat." If that's true, I am nothing except a perfectly composed, tasteless formula engineered by someone else.

I have an act nobody can see through. I know all the right moves, all the right smiles, and all of the perfect lies. I lie to everyone that cares because I don't want them to worry, to hover. But what scares me the most is I lie to myself right along with everyone else. I no longer know the truth, and if I do I have become so adept at denying it, I no longer know how to be honest with myself. I try so hard to make the ice look thicker than it is. STURDY, UNBREAKABLE, STABLE. I'm so afraid of them finding out how fragile the layer of ice really is. So scared that I'll lie to them, I'll even lie to myself.

-Journal Entry, March 1999

Many of my friends made attempts to visit, to be there, but after they visited once, they usually did not come back again. Either they saw I was not really there, or it was too hard for them to watch me. Whatever it was, they usually came once and then left me alone, calling occasionally. I remember two of these times very distinctly.

The night of my birthday, just two nights after I got the feeding tube, several of my friends showed up at the house, unannounced, unexpected. I was making dinner for myself, trying so hard to get excited about eating it, and I looked up and saw headlights in the driveway. I knew who it was. I ran to my room, mortified. How should I act, what should I do? Oh God, they were going to see IT. I was crying and my mother was trying to coax me out of my bedroom before they got to the door. I knew how to swallow my feelings and I was good at it, so despite my fear I choked down my tears, wiped my eyes and put on my smile. I walked out of my room and there they were with cards, flowers, a box of brownie mix, and smiles. The smiles faded. They looked at me and tried not to stare, but who wouldn't? I had a tube coming out of my nose, and a huge square piece of tape holding it to my cheek. It was the culmination of my utter and complete humiliation. Tears burned my eyes and the back of my throat was tight in addition to the pain from the tube. Oh God, what had I come to? I thought I was strong, and everyone thought I was perfect, and now they could see that I was not. They saw how terribly wrong they were and I saw how terribly weak I was. I could not cry in front of them though, I had so little left to hold on to; I could not entirely lose my dignity in front of them.

"Does it hurt?" *Good*, I thought, *let's talk about it like it's a scrape or something.*

"No." *Yes, it's excruciating to have all of you seeing me like this, it hurts like hell. Yes, it hurts my throat and my tummy, but I'm not going to tell you that. Why would I? Please go away, please, if you really care.*

"Well, we miss you."

"Yeah, I miss you guys too." *Who do you miss? I'm blank, there's no one here except a sad, sad girl. But you can't know anything about her.*

"Happy birthday."

"Thanks." *Did you say happy birthday? Did I hear that correctly? I am so sorry. I know this is awkward for you too.*

"We'll come visit again, and call."

"Okay, please do." *Please don't.* And they didn't, they didn't come visit again. Sometimes they called, and I know they cared, but I was unreachable.

The other visitor was my toughest competitor from our cross-country team. We had a quasi-friendship that was laced with competition. She, too, brought me a birthday gift. It was lotion, really nice lotion. I had had the feeding tube for a few weeks, and at first it was a bit easier to see her, maybe because time had passed and it was just one person. We sat on the ground by each other and she proceeded to confide in me that she thought she might also have an eating disorder. It crushed me. Competition flared in me at the same time that fear gnawed at me. *Are we going to compete in this too?* She was small and thin. She talked to me and talked to me. I could not handle it, not then, not from her.

After she left, I was distraught. Part of me wanted to help her and part of me wanted to beat her in the "eating disorder game." This is yet another dark side of eating disorders that I hated to admit. I constantly compared myself to others. Was I smaller than she was? Did I run as much as she did? I wasn't such a nice person, was I? I wanted to compete with people even over sick things. What about her welfare? The only thing that saved me from feeling completely evil was that I did care about her. I hurt for her as I hurt for myself. It was easier to hurt for her though, because she deserved my sympathy. Somehow I did not.

I sat by the fireplace with my tube for months. Gradually, I started to go out of the house to do errands with my mom or dad. After appointments we would sometimes go to my favorite grocery store, or have coffee. I had a strong desire to eat following appointments. I would be infused with reason for an hour and walk out of the office resolved that this week would be the turning point for me. It never really lasted. Yet, the few minutes of feeling better were valuable. I clung to them. They were my hope that maybe one day I would be normal again. That I could still be normal again. I felt crazy most of the time. Teetering on the cliff of sanity, barely holding on. I knew I was sick. Stepping outside of myself and seeing that was not difficult; being inside myself and feeling helpless to change was very difficult. Eventually I learned to recognize that anorexia was not me; it was something that plagued me.

I was not sick, my *mind* was not sick. Rather, there was something that had captured me and taken control. So often my therapist would tell me, "Don't let it become *you*, Rae. It's not you. If you succumb to it, you give it power." So many times the lines between my anorexia and me blurred and turned fuzzy and I would flounder in the confusion. Sometimes, I threw myself wholeheartedly into the confusion and let myself wallow in it. In these times I could pretend I was fine, even when I had the feeding tube. I believed that there was nothing wrong, and I honestly could not figure out what all the fuss was about. I would squirm under the attention I was receiving, like a child playing hooky who begins to feel guilty when her parent shows her concern.

I remember a session with my counselor during one of these times. He asked me how I was doing, as he usually did at the beginning of our meetings. I remember I was feeling especially comfortable with myself that day. I felt like I had reached an easy balance where, if I could keep things the same, I could manage things. I told him this and thus concluded that I felt good and things were going just fine, truly. He looked at me for a moment with his clear blue eyes, then said, "So, you're feeling complacent." His abruptness took me aback. I could not respond. I did not know how. I was mad. I was mad at how he took away my sense of peace. I was mad because deep down I knew he was right and I did not have the energy or desire to face it. There were so many times that I tried to talk my mom and dad out of taking me to those appointments. I would tell them I was fine or that I did not know what to talk about. I would tell them that the counselor was not working for me. Then, as a last resort, when I knew they were not changing their minds, I would cry. I walked out of those appointments with headaches, splitting headaches. Sometimes there was relief, or a resolve to do better, but no matter what, there was always a headache.

XII
Losing the Tube

I was on the feeding tube from January until May. It could have been longer, but a mishap helped me out. That May, my sister was scheduled to fly to Hawaii with the family for whom she babysat. She wanted me to come. I still had the feeding tube and worried what it would be like. I still possessed very little energy, and it was tiring to be in public with my feeding tube. There were always questions and inquisitive looks. Everyone thought it would be good for me. For some unknown reason, I decided to go, feeding tube and all. We stayed in plush resorts that served amazing buffets of food every morning. Somehow, I felt safe in all of the anonymity. I did not worry about seeing people I knew, and I felt safe knowing that I could lie to strangers when they asked questions, and they did. I told them I had stomach problems and my feeding tube was helping to supplement my nutrition.

I was safe in my lies in the mass of strangers. I could almost ignore my problem, except for the buffets of food and the horrible anxiety that I encountered at each meal. There was always fear--fear of losing control, fear of gaining weight, fear that the correct foods would be there or that there would not be enough of them. I had to face this anxiety three times a day when we all sat down to eat, and each encounter with food brought new anxiety and fear. I had gained ten pounds on the feeding tube by this point and the new weight was already painfully noticeable to me. I could not imagine carrying more weight.

All the while, I was helping my sister with a three-year-old and a one-year-old. They would wake up very early in the morning due to the time change, and my sister and I would get up with them. We went on hikes over the lava rocks, and the kids always wanted to be carried. I did it all. I refused to look weak in any way. Then, one day, while I was changing his diaper, the baby reached up, curious as usual. However, this time his curious little fist caught a hold of my feeding tube and pulled. As he jerked at it, I felt the strange sensation of the tube going up the back of my throat, tickling my esophagus. I quickly grabbed his hand and pried the tube from his grasp before he pulled it out any further, but I knew something was wrong. I went to my sister, and told her what had happened.

My heart was racing. I did not know whether to be elated that the tube might have to come out or to be scared. I called my doctor, and after a number of calls back and forth between the hospital and the doctor, he told me the tube had to come out. He said that if it had been pulled out enough, it could suffocate me when I put liquid into it because the liquid would go into my lungs rather than my stomach. He instructed me to lie down on a bed, relax my throat and pull the tube slowly out of my nose. I had come to depend on the tube. It was my life insurance. I did not have to decide to eat with the tube. Just put the formula in and let it drip, drip, drip into my body. I slept through the hell of putting calories in my body. I was not choosing to take care of myself, not really. What would happen to me? What if I could not eat? I was going to die. I was going to mess up and it would all go backward. They would start watching me again; they would all be breathing down my neck. I could not stand the thought. I felt panic rise in my throat, the kind of panic where I could feel the airways in my throat closing, my body clenching, and my heart racing. I swallowed the panic, and a part of me, the Voice part, was brimming with excitement. No fulltime babysitter! No more weight gain! I could go back to how I was. No more dumping leftover formula into the sink before anyone woke up.

I walked into the bedroom of our suite. I was surrounded by plush carpet and ornate furniture in a resort for the rich and famous. It all felt so surreal. How did I get to this point? My sister was playing with the kids in the next room and I was all by myself, staring at the bed, knowing what I had to do. I lay down and slowly, slowly started pulling the tube out of my nose. I could feel it moving in the back of my throat, sliding in the back of my nose. Then I tasted the stomach acid, burning in the back of my throat. I kept pulling, hand over hand, like I was climbing a rope. The tube felt miles long but it was no more than two feet. When I finished pulling the tube out, I balled it up and threw it in the trash. God knows what the maids must have thought when they cleaned the room. I walked out of the suite and helped my sister take the kids and our bags to the car and we drove to the next resort.

It was so strange. There was so much going on inside me, yet I kept going. I did not let anybody know how scared I was. I did not ever let anybody know much, for that matter. I spent my energy creating a facade for times like these. Times when I was scared of the emotion that would come out, times when I could not be sure about my strength. There are acceptable ways for a person to behave, and I was painfully aware of this. I wanted to scream; I wanted to cry. I wanted to tell someone how excited I was and how terrified I was. I wanted to have the most outrageous outburst. That would have been a true reflection of my feelings. Instead, I remained composed, calm, serene almost. The questioning looks from my sister were deflected by a reassuring, yet fake, smile that said, "I'm okay. Really." It didn't occur to me to tell someone how I really felt. I never wanted to cause any undue upset on my account, or risk saying how I felt and be misunderstood. I didn't want to make a scene, to draw attention to myself. In order to accomplish this, I couldn't indulge my feelings or lose control. The answer was in perfection.

XIII
Perfect

Is this what I am? A person governed and inhibited by her outward appearance? What went so wrong inside me? While I know the depth of my soul, I view myself so shallowly. How do I get past the overtaking judgment that causes me to retreat and mourn over something so very concrete, so material, so shallow. My body doesn't make me, other people don't make me. My soul, my spirit is what completes me. Yet I can't seem to get past the box in which I am contained. There are no windows that see out and none that can see in. The mirror only reflects my body, the smile reflects my soul. I have no smile. Where's my smile? How does appearance gain so much control over me and have such a tight grip on my hand? There's so much more to show. There's so much more to me, and I don't let anyone see. Instead my thoughts and fears hinder me, and I become locked in my cage with no one to pull me out and only me to keep pushing myself back in. How does one change their ways? How do you go about accepting yourself?

I'm a bird that clips my own wings so that I never have to fear that I will fall. Instead, I know with certainty if I try that solo flight with no feathers to make me light, I will plunge to the ground. So I stay where I am, safe, while all the time I know if I had just let those feathers grow, I would be soaring through the sky, so, so high.

If only you could see the fear inside me. And if only I knew what you may have been through. Then maybe we could understand that you and I are just human. And maybe our fear would dissipate, and we would be left with only ourselves. Then maybe we would know that we had the same fears and that we have both felt inadequate at times.

Then maybe you wouldn't be so high up on that pedestal, and I would stop trying to be there with you. Maybe you and I, we would finally meet at the same level. I could really see you and you, you could really see me. I want you to see me. That would be the ultimate freedom. We could finally be a human with a human sharing our humanity, and I would be free...

-Journal Entry, April 1999

I needed to be perfect, and to me perfection meant being composed and strong so that no one was ever inconvenienced or disappointed. If you were perfect, you faded into the background, unobtrusive. Of course, my ideal didn't allow for being human. I started to call this way of acting the "Perfect Game." I struggle with this always. When expectations pile on and your image is one of competence and intelligence, you will fight to keep that image. You will fight because maybe if you can be like that image, you will eventually become that image. If I lost that, everyone would see my secret, *I'm not perfect, far from it.* To let people down like this, to shatter their expectations, this was intolerable to me. As long as I thought no one knew I had anorexia, my anorexia made me strong. Yet, the feeding tube screamed my secret to everyone, "She screwed up! She has problems!"

Why was that so hard to accept? Because no one seemed to believe I had problems, and I wanted to believe that too. So if I perfected my appearance and governed myself closely, I could ensure that I would never let anyone down, even myself. There were so many feelings trapped inside me. They appealed to me and I hammered them down, pounded them deep into myself; I was cruel to them, merciless. I had to be, because everything was at stake. *Don't lose control Rae, you'll lose everything.* But, of course, living like this took its toll. The worst part was that I became so good at squashing those feelings, at holding up my facade, that I lost the boundaries between what was real and what was not. I lost the ability to know what I felt. I lost myself. Living the lie killed me.

Sometimes I wonder what would have happened if I had learned how to voice my feelings, how to be real just a little bit sooner. The tube was not only my life insurance, it was a sign that said, "I'm not perfect, and I don't have to try to be perfect any longer." While it did not fix everything, or necessarily anything, it did provide relief in big ways. With the tube out, the pressure to be perfect was back. It weighed on me, yet it felt so good to walk around and *look* normal. It felt good to be able to play the perfect game again. There were many contradictions flying around inside my mind, as always.

I did eat that week. In fact, some days I ate three normal meals a day *and snacked*. I now found myself constantly anxious around food. Every time I had to eat it, be around it, I felt fear. I *wanted* to eat so badly, but I feared losing control. What if I started to eat and I could not stop? Food was not food anymore, but a discipline, a source of fear, a traumatic experience most of the time. I tried to remember when it had happened, when it had changed. I could remember as a twelve-year-old eating whole packs of ramen noodles, peanut butter milkshakes, and pizza—all things I felt I could no longer *touch*. It seemed like my memories were of another person. Nonetheless, I made it through the week feeling liberated and haunted by my liberation. I was not sure I was ready for it.

We returned home and I put my foot down. I refused to get the feeding tube put back in despite my doubt that I would actually eat. I even insisted on returning to school for the last few weeks of the semester. I was always pushing myself and my boundaries. I wish I could say that I wanted to get better at this point, but deep down I did not. Deep down I wanted to lose weight again, and that is why I did not want the feeding tube. I was sick of my behavior, my obsession, but that did not mean I was ready to let go of it. I was driven by my need for perfection and for achievement—that is what my eating disorder was to me. It was my striving for perfection. Never mind that I had blown my cover and the people that loved me knew that I had an eating disorder. Never mind that every day that I did not eat I lost more of myself. Never mind that my eating disorder took away my potential, my life. This was not rational, but it had never been about rationality. I went back to school after I got back from Hawaii.

I felt all the old, familiar pressures begin to creep back and settle on my shoulders like they had never been gone. There was the familiar nagging in the back of my mind saying "You should be studying, no time for breaks." The tension was back, and once again I was afraid to be myself. I was not sure I knew how to be myself. How does one go about letting go of all her barriers, fears, and feelings of obligation? It seemed that if a person were to do that, expectations, standards, and discipline would go too. I was so tired, and there was so much work I needed to make up.

I felt overwhelmed by the amount of work I had to do and the amount of time I had missed. Taking time to enjoy myself was anxiety provoking. What if it made me lose focus and I became lazy? I told myself that that was why I had to go back to school, I was losing focus. I wanted to shrug this weight off my shoulders, yet at the same time, I embraced it. It made me feel like I was accomplishing something. If I was not successful, what was I good for? I knew it was this way of thinking that had led me astray, and I wished I could change it, but it was a part of me. I had operated this way my whole life. In addition, this terrible feeling was validated by my observation that everyone around me that did well operated this same way.

My worth was grounded in my achievement. I was a puppet whose strings were controlled by everyone's hopes for me. I was like a dog trying to please my master. I did all kinds of tricks, knowing that if I got a treat I had done a good job and my master was pleased. I was addicted to this positive feedback. I depended on others for it because I couldn't give it to myself. My worth felt directly related to how much I pleased others. Inactivity was not just about laziness, it was empty space where I received no pats on the back, no accolades, and in the silences, in the quiet times, there was nothing from me to fill this space. I was who everyone thought I was, that was all, that was it. I knew there was more, I knew I was slowly killing myself. I had no idea how to bring "me" back to life.

XIV
Back to School

I was back at school for three or four weeks before the year ended, feeling disoriented, like being jolted awake after nodding off. I walked out of one strange world into another. No one knew how disoriented I felt, how lost I was. I did my work and took on my duties as high school secretary, a position I had been elected to before I left school. There was a mix of awkwardness and relief in being back at school. In some ways, I felt closer to normal, but in other ways I realized how far away normal was. I went to school. I did my work. I felt a sense of independence that had long been taken away from me. But I had a hard time relating to my friends; while I spent time with them, I felt alienated and distant.

As I walked through the hallways, it felt like a chasm of time separated two very distinct time periods in my life. I felt haunted. There were so many reminders, so many associations that beckoned to me. I would walk through certain parts of the hallways and remember vividly how cold I used to be all of the time. Granted, I still got cold, I was still supposed to be gaining weight, but now I had some strength. Those memories tugged at me because although I knew I was working toward being in a better place, I did not really want to move forward; I wanted to go back. I did not want to feel my pants around my waist. I wanted to feel light. I romanticized about how I used to feel. Never mind that I never felt all that light. I had been too tired to feel light.

At school, I approached everything with the same intensity and conscientiousness that I always had; it looked like I had never missed a step. Except that I had, and everyone knew that I had, and it killed me to know that they knew. There were many rumors. Some people thought that I had gone to Hawaii for three months for no good reason. Others thought I was in intensive care in the hospital. Nonetheless, they saw the changes in my body weight, and this seemed to clarify the story for many, or at least I thought it did.

I was very aware of my weight gain and the change in my appearance. I cringed as people looked at me. I would imagine that they were thinking, "Wow, she gained some weight!" or "Look how fat she got!" It never occurred to me that I had gained only ten pounds at this point. To me it felt like fifty. It felt like I was wearing my imperfections, my insecurities, and my flaws on my sleeve. It was like walking around with a sign announcing my weakness to the world. I was in a state of utter humiliation. It did not matter what people said. If someone said, "You look really good, Rae," I interpreted it as, "You have gained a lot of weight and I notice it." Or if they said, "You look so much healthier," I heard this as, "You look fat."

My self-consciousness was agonizing. I could not transcend what I thought people were thinking. It was all that mattered. I stopped wearing jeans, then I stopped wearing pants that showed my body. I wore loose skirts and long-sleeved shirts. I had gone from wearing long-sleeved shirts to cover my overly thin arms to wearing long-sleeved shirts to cover my "fat" arms. It seemed like no progress at all.

Every day is a task, every thought equals fear, dread, or sadness, and every word is depressed. I'm sick of myself. I'm ashamed of myself, and I'm totally and utterly wrapped up in myself. I can't escape my mind, and I can't live with it anymore. There must be a release. Where's the key to my locked door? Where's the secret to my happiness? I'm screaming inside. God, get me out of here. Get me out of my mind, and out of this body. It's madness and I can't stop it. It's in my head and I hate myself for it, but even more I hate my casing. I hate my BODY! It betrays me as I betray it. I hate that my head swims with how trapped in my own mess I am. I want to move on, but I'm stuck in a rut and it sucks me in. Please help me solve the puzzle that will take away this pain, and relieve this horrible shame. I've been here for much too long.

-Journal Entry, June 1999

My eating disorder was my constant companion before I was forced to leave school, and when I came back, it was my companion in a new way. I was getting better physically, and yet mentally I was not sure that was what I wanted. I was so sick of the all-consuming thoughts. I was tired of restricting food, of second-guessing what "normal" eating was. Now, when mealtimes came, I worried I would lose control. I worried that I would eat everything on the table and still not want to stop. I worried that, because I was gaining weight, everything would go to hell—my eating, my control, my power, all of it would be gone. Sometimes when I came home from school, I would be by myself, and I would get so scared that I would buckle under the fear and do exactly what I was most afraid of. I would eat all night long. I started getting small snacks, putting the snack on a plate and then throwing the rest of the package away. I would throw away partial boxes of cereal or candy, for fear that maybe I *would* actually eat all of it.

Before, I knew how to punish myself. Now, I learned how to truly hate myself. I went from a robotic, unfeeling, stoic shell to a mass of feelings that I could not understand and did not want to understand. I was confused. I did not know who I was. I did not know what I felt. I could not even read my hunger cues anymore. I was completely and utterly out of touch with myself. Gaining weight had made this painfully apparent because suddenly I had the energy to feel, to want, and to be aware of the world around me, even though I could not quite seem to engage in it.

I can have every good intention and tell myself with the utmost conviction that I will change my life, but I haven't found the secret that will make me follow through. I can be what everyone wants me to be. I can be loved by many, but I can't love myself. Why can't I feel free? Why can't I be true to myself? With each passing day, my hope slips further away and I'm afraid that someday I will be a faint memory. Then my life will truly be my hell, and the circle will complete itself. And what if I stay here? What if this never goes away? Will this be my forever? Will I never find what it's like to love life and love myself? Where did everything go wrong? When did I let myself get away? I wish I could understand exactly where I am, and I wish I could see why I can't make a promise to me. I write this to myself, but somehow I know it won't help. So where do I go from here?

-Journal Entry, August 1999

XV
First Loves

Brisk fall days, warm-ups and nervousness, fatigue and highs.
You were a part of it all.
Hot summer days, dizziness and accomplishment.
You were there.
You lightened it all and made it so much less.
You haunt me like a scar on the face,
unavoidable and inconcealable.
And I will never forget you.
You are in my mind,
unavoidable and inconcealable.
Of everything, why was it you?
And why don't you fade?
And why can't I forget?
You, my protector and my pain.

-Journal Entry, September 1999

I remember my therapist telling my family that the feeding tube was necessary because if I dropped below a certain weight, he would lose me. I did not know what he meant by that, but later I figured it out. He meant that he would lose any ability to reach me, to make me *hear* him. I did not care about anyone. I was aware of them, I faintly felt their love and support, but it didn't *touch* me. I knew my mother was on Paxil. I knew my family was in chaos trying to figure out what to do, but I did not care. Yet, as my weight came back and my energy came back, so did my feelings. I lost my mechanical, robotic way of operating. I started to cry, I started to feel my isolation, my emptiness. It was difficult to see this change as positive in any way. The feelings I had been protecting myself against started to come, flooding me, while my defenses were down.

I had built a shell around myself, and my eating disorder kept the bad feelings from penetrating. When I finally started to cry, the sadness and despair were so deep that it frightened me. Feelings would come rushing out in bursts disproportionate to the small crisis I might be experiencing. It was not easy; often I was humiliated, but in many ways the pain felt good. I saw the world outside of me, and for the first time in a long time I wanted to be a part of it. I wanted to be present, I wanted to live rather than simply exist. Beyond this realization, my emotions were utterly confusing to me.

In the beginning stages of my recovery, I started to date a boy. It was the first relationship of any kind that I had allowed myself to be in following the feeding tube, and it felt good. He was kind and compassionate, and while we never talked too deeply about anything, it was just what I needed. I loved him for the way he made me feel. He accepted me, and beyond that it did not matter. He was easygoing with a lighthearted kind of acceptance, and it was refreshing for me. He was the first person outside of my family I talked to about my eating disorder. He honestly admitted that he did not understand, but that he was sorry for my pain. I will never forget his kindness. He gave me a glimpse of what it was to be alive, and through our relationship I gained a bit more courage to let go of my eating disorder. Our relationship showed me the positive side of feeling, the good parts that I had been missing, and it gave me the motivation to keep pushing and moving forward in my recovery. I began to realize that my eating disorder blocked out the good along with the bad.

I started to feel a tiny bit of distance from the haunted girl I had been a few months earlier. The feeling came and went, and on many days, my situation seemed as bad as it had ever been. But I began to separate myself. It was like breaking up with a longtime friend whom I knew was not good for me—a destructive relationship, but a friend all the same. My eating disorder, although cruel and harsh, was my protector from the pain life brought.

At the end of my junior year of high school, I knew I had turned a corner, but recovery was still a long time in coming. Making the decision to try to recover is just the beginning. Like a child growing up, it is hard to track from day to day how much the child changes until one looks back. Seeing the child every day, one does not grasp how much she is changing and growing. It was much the same with recovery—the process is so slow that only now, in looking back, do I see that progress.

Life continued to come at me. That summer I went to a leadership camp for high school government officers. I also went to Girl's State—a camp where girls from all over the state spent a week setting up and running a mock government. Both weeks were extremely difficult. Mealtimes were three times a day. I had to eat in front of people, and there was food everywhere. I could not focus on anything but how I could avoid the dreaded mealtimes.

It was during these camps that I realized how much of a coping mechanism my eating disorder was. Whenever there was too much to deal with, I let my mind be consumed with thoughts of food and exercise. Everything else simply faded away; nothing else mattered. What a blissful way to brush off the pain, the emotions, the concerns, the pressures. I was too conscientious and too aware of everyone else to give myself reprieve from the worry. I managed to focus these feelings on something inert and unemotional, food. When I was sad for some "unexplainable" reason, I would criticize myself, my body, my lack of discipline concerning food, and my weight gain. I would fill my thoughts with so much disgust for myself that my real sadness would be blocked. It was like pinching my arm so that I could forget about the pain elsewhere in my body—it did not take the pain away, it distracted me from it.

Eventually I realized that this reprieve was not really a reprieve, and I had to slowly leave where I was. However, when I say slowly, I mean slowly. My eating disorder was like sucking my thumb, which I did until I was six. It was embarrassing and I knew I should quit, but nevertheless, whenever there was a spare moment at school when

I could hide behind a corner and suck my thumb, I took it. I slowly weaned myself, telling myself I did not need to do it. When I finally gave it up, it felt like such a big loss. It was a comfort to me; I could not remember *not* doing it. Of course, when I did quit many things got better. There was no more having to hide my secret. I felt grown up and proud of myself. Yes, my eating disorder was a lot like sucking my thumb. Except there was not quite as much pride in recovering from my eating disorder; that did not come for a long time. Instead, there was mourning and immense pain.

What was it that I could not bear to face? I believe that *part* of my pain was my utter lack of self. It seemed like all of my life there had been an agenda for me, unstated, but nonetheless it existed. As a child, I was always praised as if I were abnormal, above par, outstanding. I was made to feel as if perfect and extraordinary were the only acceptable ways for me to be. Somehow it was my destiny to be great, to be someone. This did not allow for mistakes. This idea that I *must* be perfect was an ingrained way in which I operated, and everyone around me reinforced it. I was on a pedestal that I did not want to be on, yet I killed myself to stay there.

Why? I do not know. Probably for love. Accomplishment and perfection won me love. Yet, on some level, I knew how empty that love was. This was my pain. As I realized this, I shied away from praise and expectations because they locked me into a life that I could not and did not want to live. I hated feeling like I was on a pedestal. I oscillated between feeling like I was on one, or that everyone else was on one and I was not. It was a feeling of having to be perfect, but knowing inside I was not. I felt utterly inadequate compared to others, and ultimately, unlovable.

I could never escape feeling that there was an agenda for me that was not my own, even before the eating disorder began. In my sophomore year, I tried to rebel against this by smoking pot and cigarettes, getting drunk, lying to my parents and skipping school. Every time I came home with my head down-ashamed, guilty, and regretful. I was a puppet and, in a way, while the anorexia muted this pain, it also gave me a way to assert myself. I felt that my life was out of my control, that I was helpless, hopeless and lost, but by choosing not to eat, I could dance to my own drum, however tiny the beat. It was this tenacious part of me that would not surrender to everyone else's desires. I found that it was I who could ultimately decide the course of my life, whether it was to live or die.

My eating disorder made me feel capable of rebelling, of being different, wild, irresponsible—my own person. I was asserting myself in a way that was not outright rebellion, so I never felt ashamed for disobeying. My eating disorder allowed me to have control over my life and my choices. It said to others, "You don't own me or know me, you never will. I can make decisions for myself even if you don't like those decisions." It was my confirmation that I still possessed a will of my own. Yet, what a paradoxical way to assert this. In trying to gain power, I lost my power to yet another thing, another pressure, another voice that was not my own. It was an evil trick, an unfair trick. It was heartbreaking when I began to discover all of this. My seemingly strong foundation began to crumble beneath my feet and I was left searching, scrambling—ignoring that the foundation was crumbling while looking for firmer ground.

XVI
Tentative Embrace

That same summer I took a job at a bakery. I needed something to fill my time. I knew that participating in sports my senior year would not be allowed, and I didn't want to think about the summer training that I wouldn't be doing. A job would give me structure and purpose, and I thought it would help immensely. I was baking six hours a day. I loved baking although I was not sure whether truly I loved it or if I was still feeding my obsession.

When I would not let myself eat, nothing pleased me more than to see someone else eating, especially something I had made for them. I read later that this is common for people with eating disorders and it surprised me. I was never quite able to articulate why making food for other people gave me such a good feeling, but when I read this it all made sense. I wanted to eat, and I derived vicarious pleasure by making food for people and seeing them eat it. It satisfied me somehow. I think that is what my baking job was about initially. The real problems started to occur when I began to eat what I baked.

I went several months without eating at work, but gradually I started to sample bites of broken cookies, brownies, and muffins. I hated myself for it and would punish myself by eating more rather than stopping. I would go home depressed and irritated with myself, feeling utterly hopeless. I remember driving home one day. It was hot and I was wearing a tank top. I happened to look at my arm and the size of it startled me. It was no longer sinewy and bony, it had flesh, enough fat to pinch. I did pinch it; I ran my hand up and down my arm, horrified. I was so ashamed of myself, so embarrassed that I could not even cry. I choked everything down and drove the rest of the way home blank, mortified by myself, scared shitless. I didn't wear a tank top again, not for a good two and a half years.

This was the start of a new phase of recovery for me. My hatred for myself grew exponentially over the next year, and my full-time job became devising ways to cover my body, trying to disappear as I had earlier. I stopped wearing pants when I thought my legs were too big. If I did wear pants, they were either baggy scrubs or pajama pants, never anything that fit or that I could even remotely feel on my body. At my worst, I went to visit my brother who was going to school in Tucson, Arizona. It was May, right before my high school gradua-tion, and the weather was already nearing 100 degrees. I dressed like I was still in the Northwest, getting through the last stages of winter. I insisted on wearing long skirts, long sleeves, and a jacket that hid the somewhat fitted shirt I wore. I insisted that I was not hot even as sweat made me sticky and wet under my jacket. I could not get past the self-consciousness and the mortification that I felt about my body.

I am not sure which part of the eating disorder was worse-for me or for my family. Was it the painful disappearance of my spirit and my body, or was it the passionate, terrible vengeance with which they came back? By this, I do not mean that as I recovered I fully embraced my autonomy and became fiercely independent. No, I struggled with feelings that I did not want to have. I struggled with a developing identity that I was not sure I wanted to develop, and I struggled with a body and eating behavior that I was positive I did not want. Before, my struggle had at least been a quiet one. I went through my everyday routine, never sharing my worries or my thoughts. I was dutiful and diligent in my studies and activities, too tired to be any trouble to anyone except myself. Now I was a ball of pent-up emotions mixed with new feelings waiting to be let out. I was depressed, I was angry, I was lonely, I was confused, and I was full of hatred for myself. I didn't want to let these awful, negative emotions out. So, instead, I contin-ued to try to push them away, hoping they would disappear if I could ignore them long enough.

Unfortunately, I think feelings must follow one of the laws of thermodynamics—the law that states that energy can neither be created nor destroyed. With each chemical reaction, the energy that is released adds to entropy, better known as chaos. Feelings stay, no matter where one puts them, and they wait for a time to come out, to show themselves. Just because they are ignored does not mean they go away. I had ignored a lot of feelings, and I think the corners of my mind and heart were getting too full. This, added to my improving mental health, made the perfect situation for feelings to escape whether I wanted them to or not. However, I did not know how to manage or deal with these feelings.

In sessions with my therapist, I remember crying a lot. I remember his frequently saying, "Let the feeling come, Rae. Go into the feeling. Embrace the feeling." We worked on this idea of embracing my feelings a lot during my senior year of high school. It became a joke for me I heard the phrase so much. All the same, as cheesy as it sounded, I did learn from the repetitive mantra. We spent a lot of time paying attention to my emotions. I learned that the way I cried was a physical expression of the way I tried to suppress my feelings. When I felt the tears coming, I would valiantly fight them. My shoulders would tense, I would hold my breath, the roof of my mouth would start to ache, and still I held on, wishing the tears away, urging them away. Sometimes tears would come out through choked sobs that I tried to hold back.

And then, finally, after months and months of talking about it, I let go one day. While I cannot remember exactly why, I still remember the feeling of release. I melted that day; I fell into my sadness like never before. I had never realized how much I was resisting until I let go of my resistance. I cannot describe exactly what it felt like, but it was beautiful. I did not know pain could feel so beautiful. At first, I was scared of the intensity of my sadness. I worried that my therapist thought I was too intense, overly dramatic, but then for a moment, I stopped caring and let my inhibitions melt away. It was like a wave washing over me. My body went limp, my throat opened as it relaxed and my sobs came out, my tears came, and everything rushed out. It was like dancing, really dancing, where you feel the music inside you and move to it without worrying what you look like. Crying felt right, so I let myself. It had taken more than a year since I had begun to gain weight to let this happen. A year. I held out for a whole year. No, I had held out my entire life.

That was an isolated moment for me. I am not sure I will ever feel that much blissful pain again, but I remember it and hold it dear to my heart. I can remember it and know what it is to go "into" a feeling, and I know when I am not letting myself. I still resist more than I give in. It is still difficult for me to let down, even when I am alone. Masking the pain, if possible, still feels more natural.

During this phase, I was irritated a lot. I was irritated mostly with my family. I felt myself butting heads with my mother. I felt, more than saw, patterns that I hated and that caused me problems as I was trying to find new ways to handle clearly established, yet unspoken, rules. I cried a lot. I got angry and frustrated. Many times, I asked my mother to sit down with me and reassure me that I was not losing control, that I had not eaten too much that day. Often, I would show her my food records for the day and she would then list everything she had eaten, showing me that I was eating less most, if not all, of the time. I enlisted her to fight the devil—the Voice—at these times because I knew I did not yet have the strength to fight this on my own. The Voice was still incredibly convincing in moments of weakness.

XVII
The Railroad Bridge

No matter how much healthier I began to look, there was still the longing to "go back." I hated people watching me, hovering, asking questions that you do not ask a normal person. "Did you eat today, Rae?" or in a scolding tone of voice someone would ask, "Rae, what did you eat for lunch?" There were so many little lies to tell, careful ways of choosing my words, and these answers and cover-ups were ingrained in my mode of operating. "Of course I ate lunch." *I ate an apple, and that counts.* "No, I didn't really run." *I jogged, that's not as hard as running.* I was always looking over my shoulder, always wondering who was watching me, constantly covering my tracks. I began to push for independence. Before, I had hated the watching, but I hadn't had the energy to care or to do anything about it. Now, I hated the watching and I fought it. I would usually find quiet, polite ways to dodge the questions.

More than anything, I wanted someone to confide in. I wanted to say, "No, I didn't eat lunch because when the time came it was too damn hard, and I knew I wouldn't be able to concentrate in class afterward." I wanted to say, "Every day I hate myself more and, quite frankly, I would like to die right now."

I wanted to say those things and not have someone freak out. I wanted them just to listen, hear me, hug me, and console me. One day, I lost it with my mom; I finally answered one of those ridiculous questions the way I really wanted to answer. Then, I screamed at her. I told her how tired I was of all the questions, I told her I wanted to be left alone. I told her that more than anything, I wanted her to be on my side. She responded by hugging me and saying, "I am on your side." And she was. She was, but not the way I wanted her to be. I felt my freedom being squashed, and I hated it. I was like a two-year-old pushing my caretaker's hands away as I insisted on balancing precariously on the edge of a chair. Sure they backed off, but they kept their hands out nonetheless to spot me.

On some level, this had always been my struggle with my family. Lots of times I remember feeling smothered, that their expectations were too high, too many. When I expressed feelings that threatened these expectations, I felt pushed against rather than understood, and I desperately wanted to be understood. The paradox of anorexia expressed my conundrum. It locked away my sadness at not being understood, while I expressed my pain in the destruction. I have found a bit of peace in reminding myself that my family tried the best they could to understand. I know on some level that this helped me get unstuck. I am grateful for their support.

At times, my newfound feelings overwhelmed me, and I had to find new ways to escape. I started to write more in my journal. I also found a spot to go to that gave me peace. It was a half mile from my house on railroad tracks that wended their way through the trees. There was a place where the tracks went over a small river, connecting two cliffs on either side of the stream. The tracks rested about thirty feet above the river. You could step from tie to tie and see the river below between each of them. I would go to the middle of this and sit, looking at the houses, trees, and water that were all around me. My heart started to pump when I walked out to the middle of that small bridge. I could jump, or a train could hit me; either way I could die. Maybe it was the danger that gave me a bit of peace—I felt the world open up.

From my perch, I could see the top of every house, and I felt even with the sky. It was like I had climbed a mountain and I was looking out at every obstacle that I had overcome. It was an illusion, but as I sat there, it gave me hope that someday I would be out of this blackness. As I walked over the river I felt a thrill imagining things I dared not do. Knowing that I wouldn't reassured me that I had the courage and the strength to continue getting better.

Many days when I came to the bridge, I wasn't sure I was going to make it. I sat on the bridge and promised myself to do better, knowing that tomorrow, I would probably trip and fall, knowing how hard it was going to be to pick myself up again. But in that moment, I would have a sense that I could do it. I could climb out of this hole. I would hope for patience with myself. I would hope for strength, and I would look down at the river below. I desperately hoped that no one else could see my struggle. I begged that they did not see my weakness. I told myself that one day I would feel beautiful. I told myself I was learning something about life through all of this, even though I was not certain what. I wouldn't be trapped by this world or by my mind, and I wouldn't be trapped by other people. I would be free.

My head would begin to clear. My eyes would look away from myself if only for a brief moment, and I would see a small slice of the bigger world to which I belonged. Sometimes it was comforting to know I was so small. Maybe that is what I had liked about being so thin. It was like I was disappearing, becoming nothing, and it took away the pressure.

When my mom found out where I went she started to follow me, begging me not to go. I stopped listening to her quite so much. My mom was always afraid for me, always holding all of her children close. It is probably every mother's fear to lose a child or to have a child get injured. Where in the past I would have stopped doing something when it worried her, now I stopped listening to her. I had to. I had to learn how to make my own choices despite what others wanted, especially my family. This meant taking risks, even small ones. I started to venture out of my cocoon of safety.

XVIII
Ambivalence

I fought for more freedom and for more trust. I discovered this trust had to be earned, and it could only be earned by taking care of myself. The appointments still continued, but they were not quite as frequent. I went to my therapist once every week or two. My doctor checked up with me once every month or two, and my nutritionist and I met every two weeks. My relationship with my nutritionist started to become very significant at this point.

I needed constant reassurance that I was not failing or losing control by gaining weight. She was my handle on reality, and she gave me reassurance that I was okay. When everyone else was sick and tired of talking about food, sighing and rolling their eyes when the topic came up, I could talk with her and she would empathize. Yet, at the same time, she would gently guide me to question what could be behind my obsession with food. For example, one day when I was particularly mourning my lighter form of a few months ago, she said, "Okay, what is it that you miss about being so thin? Tell me about it."

I replied, "I miss being light. It was like I didn't have to carry anything."

"Rae, listen to what you just said, do you see how metaphorical that is?"

"What do you mean?"

"'I was light. I didn't have to carry anything. Do you think that maybe you equate being thin with not having to carry any burdens?"

She was right, I did. I had never thought of it like that before and this insight gave me perspective. She pointed out simple things like this that encouraged me and, at the same time, helped me see little bits of myself that I did not see in therapy.

Therapy was difficult for me at this point. I did not have enough clarity to reflect on my bigger issues, but I knew that talking about food the entire time did not get me anywhere. My sessions were very self-directed, and most of the time I did not know which topic to talk about. It seemed like it was not in my repertoire of knowledge to *know* what topic would bring about healing. Oftentimes we sat there looking at each other as I brought up anything I could think of that was remotely safe. I figured out later, much later, that I held myself back, and this could have been one of the reasons why there was never anything to talk about. Strangely, I was not even aware of how well I kept my feelings and worries at bay. This had always been my nature to some extent, and even now I am this way. It doesn't come naturally to me to share my life and my feelings. I could blame it on being an introvert, or being scared to be vulnerable but I wish that my therapist had pushed me more at this time in my recovery. However, maybe he knew that pushing would not work.

I kept my own slow pace during recovery. Sometimes I did not like how agonizingly slow it was, but I did what I could handle, and I could not handle very much at one time. It was painstakingly gradual—probably because a good portion of me did not want to get better. At the end of the day, I was not sure if "messing up" meant eating or if "messing up" meant not eating. There was a constant battle waging in my head. *Come on, Rae, eat. You need to do this; it's good for you. Everyone wants you to; you know that it's best. It will be good. You'll get rid of this and be normal if you eat.*

And then, after I ate: *What the hell were you thinking? You weren't supposed to eat that much! Obviously if you can't control yourself, you're going to have to either stop eating or start running! What happened to you?! You used to be so strong. Now look at you. Disgusting. You can't control yourself around food!* There was such a sense of defeat after I ate. It was not usually rewarding to eat. Once I started eating, I had a difficult time stopping. It was like I was scared that I would not ever get the chance to eat again. My anxiety levels skyrocketed around food. My starved body wanted food so badly that once I started eating, it was almost devastating to stop. And yet, it was devastating to continue. I was perpetually caught in a double bind: I was damned if I did and damned if I didn't. It was not just about my body being starved. My relationship with food was an emotional one. Earlier, I did not eat to mask my feelings. Once I started to eat again, food became a way to distract myself from feeling. I "ate" my feelings away. Eating made me think about eating. It gave me something to punish myself about. If I ate too much, I could think about that all night. Then I would have a reason for feeling bad, and sometimes a reason makes everything more manageable.

My entire senior year of high school was spent in this mind frame. By the end of it, I was not sure that I had made any progress mentally, although physically I was climbing to the upper half of the healthy weight range for my height. I could run again, but it felt awful. Several times during the year, I would run six days a week for over a month in hopes of getting the blissful feeling of running back. It never came. It always felt bad. I could not adjust to the amount of weight I now had to carry. When my feet hit the pavement, it jarred my whole body, where before the impact was minimal. And I still could not eat real meals. I would have little snacks throughout the day because it felt like I was not eating. This is how I negotiated the double bind. I was scared of quantity, so if I never saw much on my plate, I could handle it. I ate things like dry cereal, fruit, and crackers. There were so many foods that I could not eat, foods that I did not deserve or could not eat without fear of "blowing up." I would not eat pizza, pasta, cheese, or bagels, and I would not drink anything except water, tea, and coffee. Any beverage with calories was off-limits.

As I was struggling through my senior year of high school, I was applying to colleges. This was a whole new problem. I did not trust myself, yet I wanted freedom so badly. I applied to colleges I wanted to go to, but I worried the whole time what would happen when I went. Would I go back to my anorexic ways when the people close to me could no longer watch me? Would I be able to cope with stress in healthy ways? I applied to the University of Oregon in Eugene, to Linnfield College in McMinnville, to Oregon University in Corvallis, and to Western Washington University in Bellingham. While I knew there were limits to the distance I could go away, I did not want to stay too close. I ended up erring on the side of too close, much to my chagrin.

I will not belabor the details. The story is called, "Crumbling under the Pressure of Family Wishes." This is where the next part of my journey lay in the path to recovery, but I was not yet ready to address it. I ended up going to Gonzaga University, thirty miles from my parents' house. I guess I can look at this as a baby step. Change didn't happen as fast as I would have liked. This marked the beginning of the separation process from my family, which was a difficult thing considering my family. I know it was painful for my mother and empowering for me. I remember telling her not to call or come over unless I made contact first. I knew it hurt her, which in turn hurt me. I did not understand what this strong feeling was, but I knew I could not ignore the need to draw definite boundaries.

XIV
Recovery

So...recovery. Is that what this is? Am I recovering? I hoped this was over. Will there always be a reason to question myself, to doubt, to wonder, and most of all to fear that maybe I am not good enough? There is always something to fix, always something to improve, and I am constantly wondering what should have been done instead. Does confidence ever become stable enough that you can depend on yourself and trust that you are complete at least in some fashion? Will a crutch always be needed? If not praise, then achievement. If not achievement, then admiration. If not admiration, then...something. And what happens when you get to the end of that list and you're it? Can you stand alone? Can you face that? And if so, can you still find a reason to continue and not hope for that list to reappear at some point? Do I reject everyone on the grounds that they may shake my already teetering confidence? Who do I let in, and whom do I spit out? How do I ever know?

-Journal Entry, September 2000

When I began college, it was strange to realize that I was surrounded by people who knew nothing about my eating disorder. Finally, in a small way, I was rid of it. No one knew my past. They would not be watching me like so many of my friends in high school had. But at the same time, I felt like no one knew me unless they knew that I was recovering from an eating disorder. It was still so raw, so much a part of me, that I did not feel like I had much else to share. If they did not know that I had had anorexia, they did not know me. It had been my life for over two years. It was my masterpiece. My piece of art that so beautifully expressed my experience of the world. Like a long-term boyfriend, it was not a relationship I could just walk away from. I was still in the relationship. There were scars, that were fresh and still healing. People had to see them; I had to explain myself. They *needed* to know if they were my friends, because otherwise, what would they really know about me? I do not think anyone realized how much I was revealing. Even I did not realize how much I was revealing about myself or I might have tried harder to hide it. I'm glad this did not happen.

Things started to change that year, yet the change was so gradual, so small from day to day that I could not really discern the change as it happened. What started with rapid physical recovery due to the feeding tube ended up being very slow mental recovery. I was not always sure I *was* recovering. There were many questions and hurts still left.

Everything felt unfinished. I felt the "healing process" had chewed me up and spit me out. Like a child who falls and scrapes her knee: crying, she goes to her mother who hugs her, kisses her knee, and then says, "There, all better. Go play." And the little girl knows something is not right; she knows she is not all better. She still feels the scrape on her knee and the wet tears on her cheeks. She is not "all better" despite what her mother said. She tries to go play, but some-how she cannot quite convince herself that what her mother said is true. I was that little girl.

Everyone saw that I was now a healthy weight and that I was eating and they said, "There, all better." Sighs of relief all around... except for me. I was still holding my breath. *God, what if I go back? What if I don't go back?* My body was healthy, but mentally I was still anorexic. I don't know which feels worse—to actually *be* anorexic or to be an anorexic stuck in a healthy person's body. Then you have to live your fear every day. It is your own personal nightmare, except you are awake for it—awake for every excruciating moment. Everyone thinks you are better, but you are not. Chewed up and spit out. Spit out into a world for which I was not sure I was ready. Maybe it was better that way; no one took the baby steps with me. No one was privy to my daily fear and dread. It was partly my fault because I didn't want anyone to know. Whenever I said my feelings out loud, they sounded superfi-cial and silly...but they weren't. The words were never adequate, never.

Everyone could breathe easier knowing I was not going to die. But it did not change the fact that I still felt like that little girl.

Well, I guess I lost my way. The way I looked must have said a thousand words, and everybody heard—I was the last to hear it though. It's odd how that works. The past few years of my life have been almost unimaginable. Who ever thought I would have a doctor, nutritionist, and psychotherapist trying to "cure" me from a fatal "disease"—my mind? I guess as I start to see things more clearly, it was a cry for help. It said, "SEE, don't you all see? I do a lot too, I'm worth a lot too! Look at what I'm doing—ALL BY MYSELF!"

I wanted to seem strong, like I didn't need help, I had things under control, when underneath I was saying, "I want to be heard. I need to be seen. I need to be respected as my own person." But I'm not sure how to say this, I'm not sure if it's okay to feel this. So instead, I'll disappear. I wanted to impress everyone, to show them how strong I was. Instead, it turned to weakness. It's odd how that works as well. They never looked until it turned to weakness. Then I was seen, then I was heard. But I had nothing to say because my strength was so far gone. I couldn't show them anything. Yet, that's when they decided to look. All of a sudden, I had everyone looking, "helping," hovering over me. But that's not what I wanted. I never wanted that. In fact, I wanted less of that.

Now, I'm getting stronger and I have a lot more to say, and now they're beginning to turn away. I'm "healthy" again, whatever that is. "Introspective," they say. "Quiet," they say. I'm on my own again. I don't have a "problem" anymore. I don't need to be tucked in at night. I'm just there, being quiet, trying to find the best way for them to hear me and still be ME. Somehow, it's hard to think that some things don't change. But I have changed. They helped me, took care of me, but nothing made them change like my "sickness" made me change. I don't know why I expected it to.

-Journal Entry, August 2000

Physical recovery comes first, then mental. Sometimes mental recovery takes much longer than the physical recovery. I hoped for a day when I would wake up and it would magically be gone, like it had never happened. Instead, I woke up morning after morning and the day before would come rushing in, like it had been waiting for me to wake up so it could come back into my consciousness to torture me. I would think of what I had eaten the day before, whether or not I had exercised, and then punish myself for all of my transgressions. I would make an impossibly perfect plan for that day to make up for the day before and get "back on track." Of course, the plan was impossible because "back on track" meant back to anorexia. I would "fail" within the first few hours and be down on myself for the rest of the day. The next morning it would start all over again.

I wish I could say, "Then one day it all changed...," but I cannot say that. I cannot say that because that miracle never happened. However, I can say that over time, it has changed. When I look back at where I was and where I am now, I can honestly say that I have gotten much better. I have been recovering each day. And each year brings more growth, more hurdles jumped. I remember the triumphs—they are small and big, but each one of them has immense value to me. I have slowly learned how to eat whatever I want again. I can now eat almost everything. I can eat pizza, pasta, even fettuccine. I can eat chips. I can eat cheese. I can eat muffins that are not low-fat. I can eat candy. This is huge for me. Each food I let myself eat again is a triumph, for it is a step closer to normal, a step toward freedom from the chains that bound me. I can eat everything that I want to eat again and it is liberating to me every time I eat something that was once forbidden to me. It has taken four years to get to this point. Four years to add back everything to my list, except maybe juice. Maybe someday I will eat these things and not even think about what a sweet indulgence it is.

I can also wear pants again. For so long after my weight gain I wore pajama pants and long skirts because they hid my body. It took me three years to wear pants, fitted pants, *real* pants. I can wear tank tops. Sometimes, not all of the time, I can walk down the street and be happy with myself, not petrified that someone is noticing my fat and degrading me in their mind for it.

I can run again. I can run, and all the muscle that my starving body consumed has returned. Four years after having a healthy weight, my lean muscle tissue began to come back, and once again I can run and it feels good. And I have learned how to run when I *want* to, not because I *have* to.

Each small physical step reflected a change that had happened on the inside as well. Eating anything I wanted was relinquishing control. It was the recognition that sometimes life is uncontrollable. It was a step in learning how to be gentle with myself. It was a step towards freedom from my self-tyranny. When I wore pants, it was like saying, "I'm not waiting anymore to be something I'm not, I accept me, and even more, it's okay to be me. I'm fine with that." Running was the triumph over anorexia, over the damned voice. Being able to run again said, "You're not going to take everything that I love from me. I will do this despite my fear of you. Why? Because I'm strong in me now and I *know* you won't take over again."

But there are still the scars. There are things reflected in my body that will never let me forget. I have the stretch marks on my sides and my hips, where, as I gained weight, my body valiantly tried to catch up on the puberty out of which I had cheated it. For a while, I had to have periodical bone scans due to having osteopenia, which meant that I had the bones of a 50-year-old. I narrowly regained my bone mass before it was too late. Three years of high calcium supplements and vitamin D made this possible. I depend on hormone replacement of some type, which will always be needed because I never got my period back. All of these will be my forever-reminders of what happened. They are comparatively small prices to pay for a life that has become richer with each passing year.

XX
Defining Recovery

My journey has left me with a new understanding of what recovery truly is. When I started writing this story, I wanted to be able to say, I *fully* recovered. No one ever says that about eating disorders. It always felt so hopeless. Sometimes girls will write me, asking for advice about how to get through the recovery process. There is always this disclaimer in their words, "I know not to hope for complete recovery. I know it never truly goes away, but how do I achieve health?" This was the disheartening message I struggled to understand too. What is the point? What is better if you are simply a healthy body walking around with an anorexic mind? Where is the motivation in that? I never found any. My motivation was to defy the odds, to achieve full recovery despite the fact that everyone assured me it was impossible.

At a certain point, I realized that it was very important for me to reconceptualize how I defined recovery. Until then, I had started to accept the idea that I would be an anorexic trapped in a healthy person's body indefinitely. I began to believe all the stories that claimed anorexics never truly get better. I surrendered to despair, and while I wished it weren't true, I didn't dare hope for more than I already had. I had learned how to control listening to the Voice. I had learned how to maintain my weight and not completely hate myself. I had learned how to exercise reasonably. However, all of these things simply maintained the outward appearance of wellness. On the inside, I knew that a major piece was missing.

I had the misconception that if all the superficial signs of health could be maintained, eventually I would no longer have anorexia, and I would no longer have the thoughts that I had had while I was anorexic. I discovered problems with defining recovery like this. I began to see that recovery is not stepping blissfully into a new world of only happy thoughts and feelings, nor is it just defined by weight gain. Recovery is learning how to manage one's life and one's painful feelings without wanting to self-destruct as a way of shielding oneself. In order to do this, I needed to know what hurt so much that self-destruction was more attractive than the pain underneath.

This is where the Voice began to make more sense to me. The Voice is not unique to eating disorders. I believe that there is a Voice in all of us. It is the empty, dark space that feels utterly alone, terrified, and worthless, and we all have our unique ways to defend and battle against this space. Mine was anorexia, but it comes in many forms. Anorexia can go away, but this dark space, the Voice, remains with us for our whole lives.

Everyone knows loneliness because inevitably, the people we care about and depend on let us down, and we, in turn, will let them down. Disappointment and the fear of losing someone's love has always been a controlling force in my life. Growing up, I believed that people went away when I disappointed or had conflict with them. In my experience, it seemed like people walked away when I was sad, angry, or depressed. So, I spent a lot of energy trying to keep these feelings to myself and trying to please other people because I equated proximity and approval with love. I did not understand my worth because my entire identity was determined by others: how they responded to me, what I did for them, whether I made them happy or not. Part of the metaphor of anorexia became more apparent. I starved my body, made it nothing, just like my sense of self was starved. I never felt like it was okay to develop an autonomous self. I believed that love and acceptance are conditional.

Really, anorexia is one response to a universal dilemma—the despair that you are alone. It is the despair that comes from feeling that who you are is unloved and unlovable, the despair that comes when you don't know how to love yourself and your voice is quashed and silenced under layers of self-doubt, fear, and muted anger. I was suffocating from despair, dying from it. I think all people feel this despair on some level.

Anorexia left its indelible mark on me and many things remain the same before and after my eating disorder. Sometimes I still punish myself, and push myself too much. Sometimes I still need to please people in order to avoid feeling the guilt and discomfort that is second nature to me. I still beat myself up when I cannot be what someone else wants me to be. There are moments that I find myself complying to keep people happy and then hating them for it. I long for connection and am sorely disappointed when a person cannot be all that I hope they can be to me. I feel helpless, my efforts feel futile, and a sense of inadequacy overwhelms me. I now realize that these things are part of my struggle with being who I am, not just with being anorexic.

I continue to strive for and gain strength over my Voice. Even if total banishment is not entirely possible, it no longer occupies a place of tyrannical power and fear over my mind. Sometimes the work it takes to face myself and understand is exhausting, but I believe that I must either commit myself to know and accept this dark space, or to give into its depths and hate myself for having such a place in my being.

Herein lies the work that will continue for the rest of my life. Is there full recovery from anorexia? I believe so. Is there full recovery from the fear that maybe we are unlovable, that maybe we aren't worth it? Is there escape and recovery from despair, the deepest sadness, the scariest solitude? Here is the perspective I now have: I have recovered from anorexia, but I will never fully recover from being human.

Epilogue

I started writing this during my senior year in college in 2004. There were weeks when everything flowed, the words were abundant, and I knew how to say what I wanted to say. Then there have been months where, try as I might, I haven't been able to write a word. Writing the last part was exceedingly more difficult than the first. I have had to resign myself to the fact that I will not be able to describe every thought, feeling, and epiphany of the last several years. I know I will look back on this one day and there will be parts I want to change. The perfectionist in me has often said, "Just stop writing now, it will never be all that you want it to be." This thought has paralyzed me at various stages of writing this story. However, as my story has circulated among college students and people affected by eating disorders, I realize that it is far better to make my story accessible to others than to wait for it to be perfect.

Since I graduated from college, the struggle to face myself has played itself out in very tangible, restless ways. My pattern is to retreat and then come back; literally and metaphorically I face myself in short, brief periods, then run like hell. Even in my running, I end up running into myself.

Upon graduating in 2004, I went to live and teach pre-school in Shanghai, China. I came back, four months early. Five months later, I took a whimsical trip to visit a close friend in Namibia, Africa. In the fall of 2005, I enrolled in a Master's program. Five months later, having completed just one semester, I transferred to another graduate program. For the next two years, I moved from apartment to apartment an average of once every four months. It seemed like there was always a logical reason behind my actions. But, in reality, behind it all was a restless spirit that was and still is desperately seeking herself and desperately attempting to lose herself all at once. Strangely, I feel I have gotten better at understanding and appreciating myself, even if my way has not always been the most efficient.

While all of my spontaneous decisions may have looked lost, scared, or misdirected, they were necessary for personal growth. I have learned that it doesn't do me any good to view life as lost or found, right or wrong. When I find myself subscribing to this belief, it paralyzes me. If I contemplate two choices, thinking, *I have to make the right choice*, no choice is made. I feel ill at ease. I feel like my very worth rests on my ability to make the *right* decision, and the fear of failure stops me in my tracks.

Growing up, I was influenced by society's and my family's value system. Success was the ultimate goal, and no one can achieve success through "wrong" decisions. "Doing" was encouraged, "being" was not. My inner voice felt squashed, my delight in life killed by all of the expectations, all of the rules and conventions. Somehow I received the message, "We don't trust that you will become a wonderful person in your own right, we must watch you and direct you." There is so much self-doubt that comes from that message.

I wrote to a therapist of mine while I was in China. In my email, I told him, "I am doing pretty well and finding Shanghai to be an energizing challenge. However, I am also finding that you cannot outrun your problems or change your life by changing your environment. I think that may have been the hope behind this decision. There is much to be learned here..." In response, he said, "Wherever you go, there you are." That phrase went through my head like a mantra for the next few months, and I decided it was time to return home with the realization that China would not help me find myself anymore than home would.

Wherever you go, there you are. And there your pains are, and your secrets, and your fears, and all of your annoying habits. You know they are there, because you carry them with you, within. I am still here. I always have been. Sometimes I see my eyes in the mirror and think, *I could hang out with you for the rest of my life. I like you.* Yet, at other times,

I writhe at the thought of me. I squirm with dissatisfaction, and fear that this is what I will have to live with for the rest of my life.

I have found out that when I stop running, when I turn around and make a step toward myself, the desire to run stays but a small sense of serenity comes as well. That serenity is compelling. I feel small pieces of it when I settle into myself. Even if the calm lasts for only a moment, I remember the experience. I know in my heart that it's not escaping myself, but embracing myself, that will make me whole.

When I returned home, I continued to feel and react to the restlessness. I felt fickle about my choices, and was always trying to re-adjust to something better. I knew logically that wherever I went, there I was, but even so, it took a while to get comfortable with the restlessness rather than react to it. I began a Master's program in Washington, and within the first semester I knew I would not be able to stay. I transferred to a different program in Montana. I made a promise to myself to stay, knowing that I may never finish anything if I kept this pattern up. I kept my promise, and two years later I completed the graduate program, and earned my Master's in Counseling. I have lived in Montana for three years now, and I am working towards licensure as a counselor.

I have encountered other women with eating disorders in the past years, and I find myself compelled to talk with them, to let them know that I understand the agony. I am at once alarmed and comforted to know that there is usually some common thread between us that is buried underneath the eating disorder. I have learned a great deal from these women. I hope that they have learned from me as well.

I also began speaking to college classes about my story and my experience. Even though the exposure at times frightens me, I find it relieving to be honest and open. Each time I share this with someone, I am reminded that we are never as alone as we might think. I am thankful for the people that love me, however best they can. I realized that my story could have ended differently, and while the journey is still not always easy, I am happy that I have a chance at being alive without the constant weight of the Voice. Linger no longer, my hell, my companion. My hands are no longer cemented over my eyes. I didn't know if that sentiment would stick when I wrote it, but I do now.

www.ingramcontent.com/pod-product-compliance
Lightning Source LLC
Chambersburg PA
CBHW060634290526
45793CB00001B/247